1940s

Ten Years of Popular Hits Arranged for **EASY PIANO**

Arranged by Dan Coates

DECADE by DECADE

Contents

Another Op'nin', Another Show 4

As Time Goes By 9

At Last 12

Because of You 15

Bewitched, Bothered and Bewildered 18

Blues in the Night 24

Chattanooga Choo Choo 28

Come Rain or Come Shine 21

Diamonds Are a Girl's Best Friend 32

Don't Fence Me In 35

Don't Get Around Much Anymore 46

Don't Sit under the Apple Tree 38

Ev'ry Time We Say Goodbye 42

Fools Rush In 49

How Are Things in Glocca Morra? 52

How High the Moon 56

I Could Write a Book 59

I'll Walk Alone 62

La Vie en rose 65

Laura 68

Mairzy Doats 74

Moonlight in Vermont 71

Moonlight Serenade 76

My Foolish Heart 79

New York, New York 82

Opus One 85

Over the Rainbow 88

Polka Dots and Moonbeams 92

Rum and Coca-Cola 98

Shangri-La 95

Skylark 102

So In Love 105

Speak Low 110

A String of Pearls 118

Swinging on a Star 115

The Syncopated Clock 122

Taking a Chance on Love 126

The Trolley Song 129

You Make Me Feel So Young 134

You'll Never Know 138

Zip-A-Dee-Doo-Dah 141

ANOTHER OP'NIN', ANOTHER SHOW

"Another Op'nin', Another Show" is the opening number from Cole Porter's musical *Kiss Me, Kate*. The incredibly successful show opened in 1948 and was the only one of Porter's musicals to run for more than 1,000 performances on Broadway. Other famous numbers from *Kiss Me, Kate* include "Tom, Dick or Harry," "Too Darn Hot," and "So In Love" (see p. 105).

Words and Music by Cole Porter
Arranged by Dan Coates

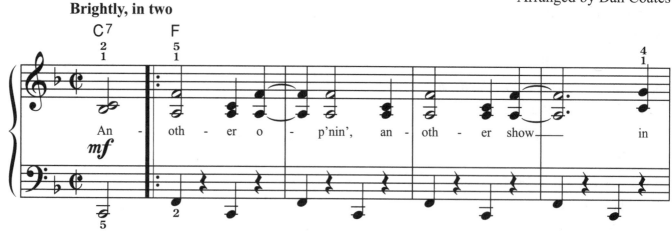

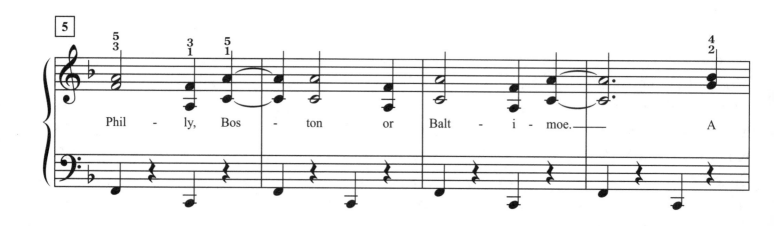

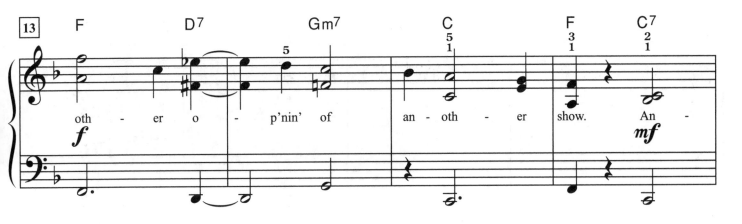

13 F — D7 — Gm7 — C — F — C7

oth - er o - p'nin' of an - oth - er show. An -

f   *mf*

17 F

oth - er job that you hope, at last, will

21

make your fu - ture for - get your past, an -

25 F#dim — C7

oth - er pain where the ul - cers grow, an -

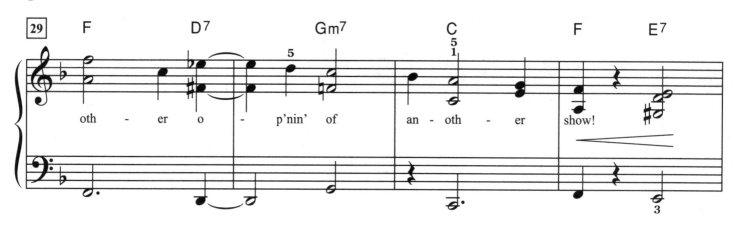

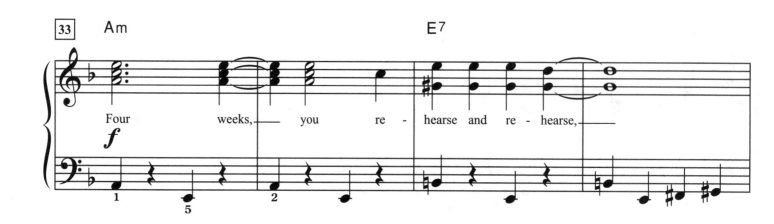

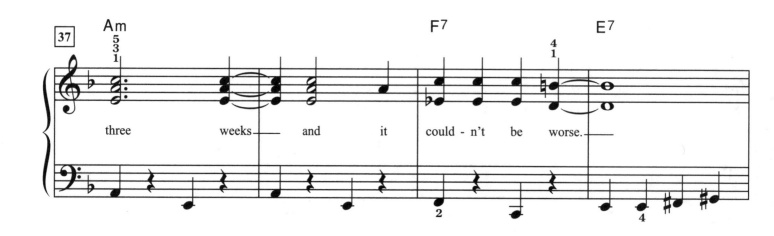

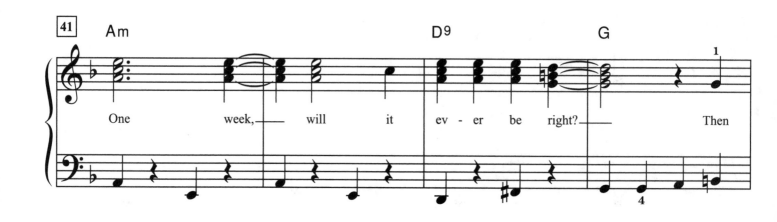

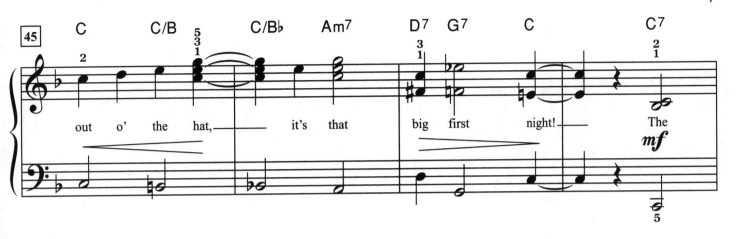

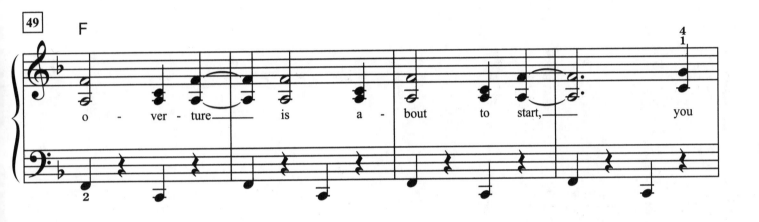

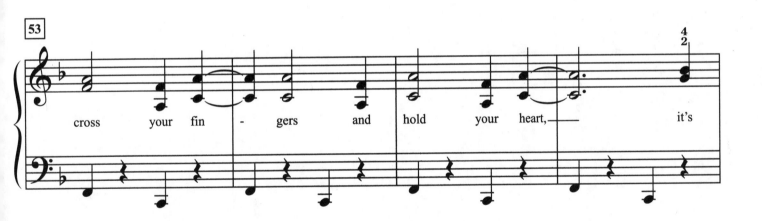

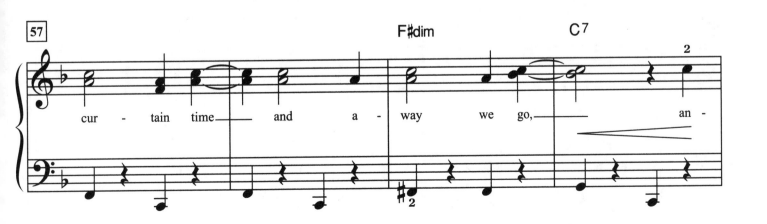

AS TIME GOES BY

"As Time Goes By" was first composed for the little-known musical *Everybody's Welcome* (1931). However, its usage throughout the classic, romantic film *Casablanca* (1942) made it famous. *Casablanca* starred Humphrey Bogart as Rick, a conflicted nightclub owner, and Ingrid Bergman as Ilsa, Rick's former lover. "As Time Goes By" was "their song" and was performed in the film by Dooley Wilson who played Sam, Rick's nightclub pianist. *Casablanca* won three Academy Awards in 1943, including Best Picture.

Words and Music by Herman Hupfeld
Arranged by Dan Coates

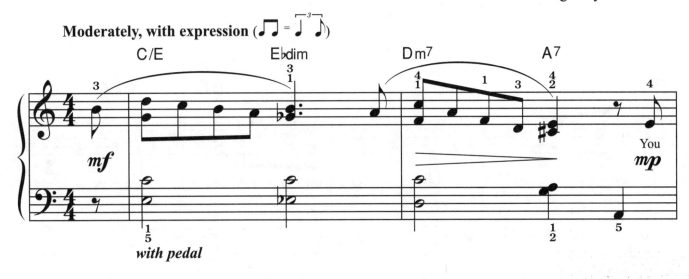

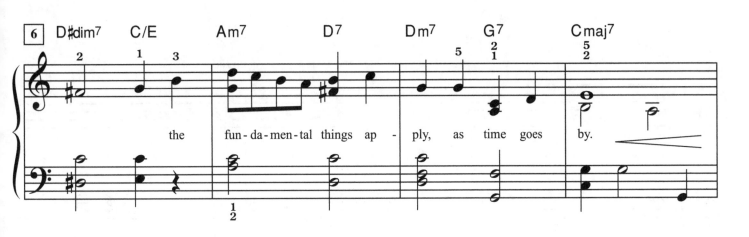

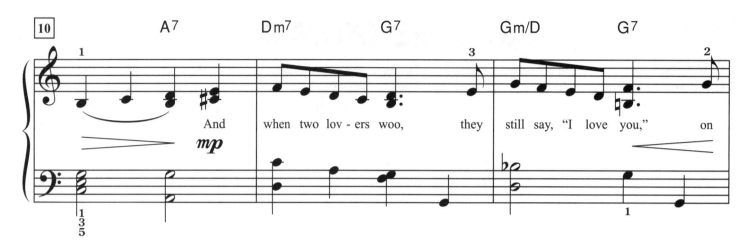

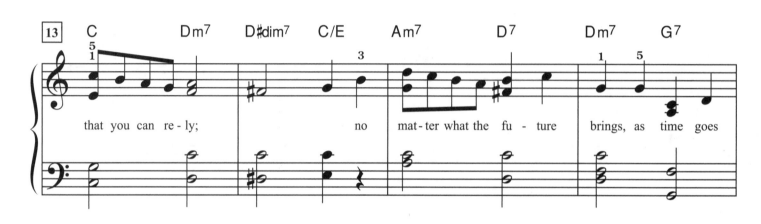

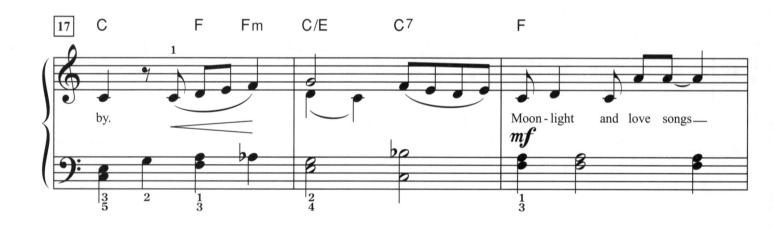

AT LAST

"At Last" was written by Mack Gordon and Harry Warren in 1941 and was a major hit for Glenn Miller and his band. However, the song is closely associated with Etta James, the famous R & B singer. In 1999 James was inducted into the Grammy Hall of Fame for her version of "At Last." It became her signature song and is frequently heard at weddings.

Music by Harry Warren
Lyric by Mack Gordon
Arranged by Dan Coates

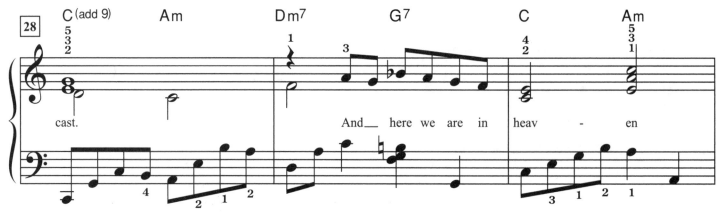

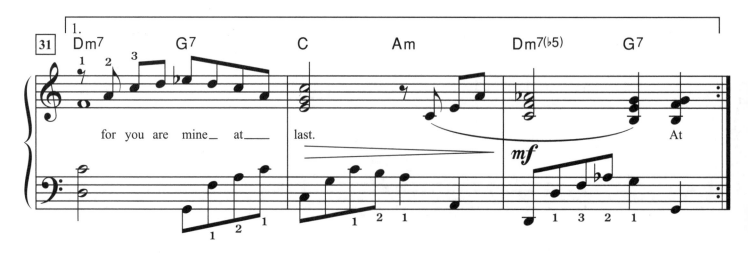

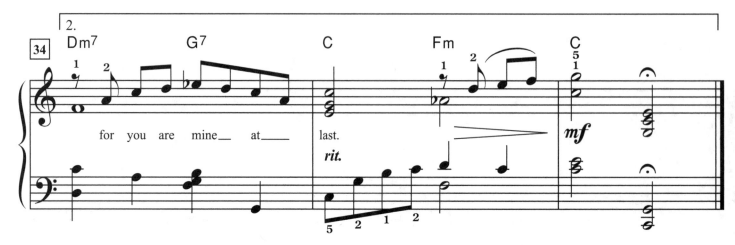

BECAUSE OF YOU

"Because of You" was featured in the movie *I Was An American Spy* and was the first major hit for Tony Bennett. His 1951 recording of it topped the Billboard charts for 10 weeks. He also recorded it as a duet with k. d. lang on his Grammy Award-winning album *Duets: An American Classic* (2006).

Words and Music by
Arthur Hammerstein and Dudley Wilkinson
Arranged by Dan Coates

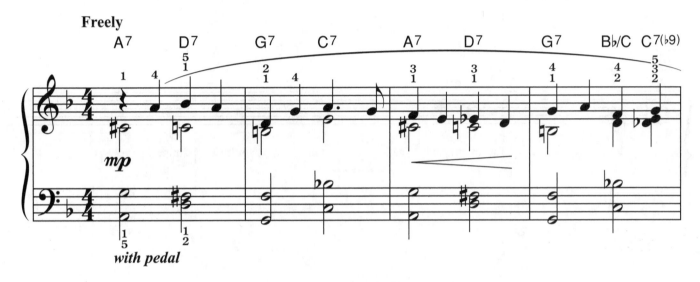

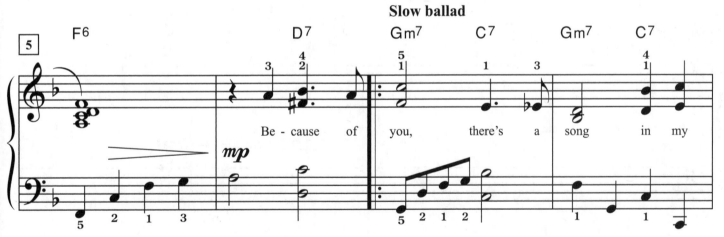

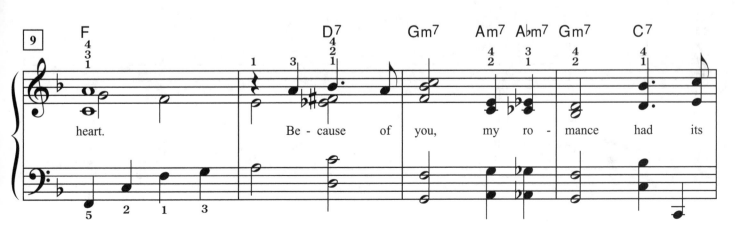

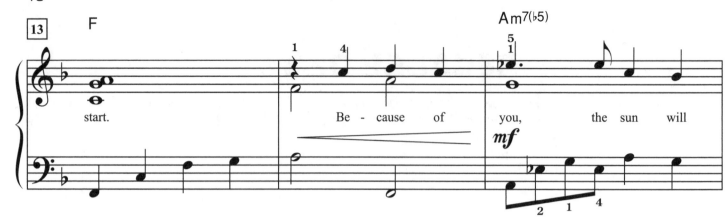

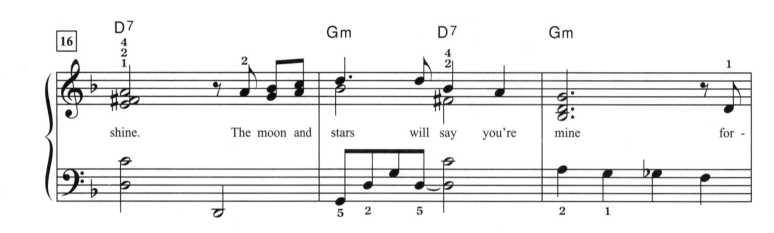

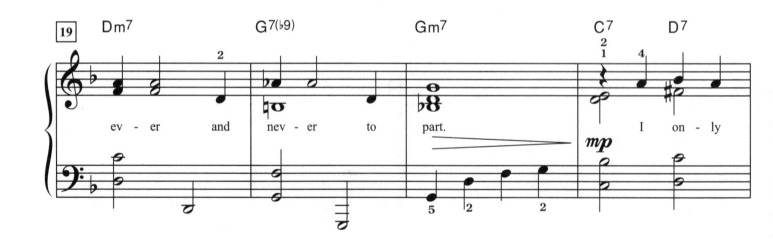

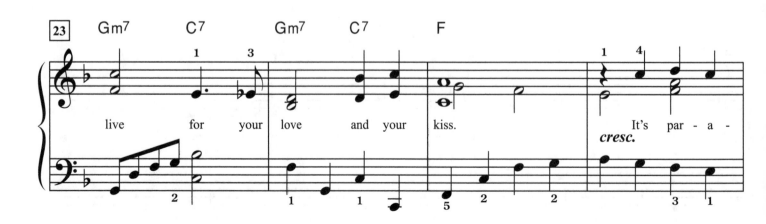

BEWITCHED, BOTHERED AND BEWILDERED

"Bewitched, Bothered and Bewildered" is from the musical *Pal Joey* (1940), which was based on the writings of John O'Hara. The music and lyrics were written by Richard Rodgers and Lorenz Hart, and it starred Gene Kelly. The original production ran for 374 performances. It was later revived in 1952, 1963 and 1976. The 1952 revival was incredibly successful and won three Tony Awards. "Bewitched, Bothered and Bewildered" has been recorded by many great artists including Doris Day, Ella Fitzgerald, Frank Sinatra, and Mel Tormé, to name a few. *Pal Joey* also featured the song "I Could Write a Book" (see p. 59).

Words by Lorenz Hart
Music by Richard Rodgers
Arranged by Dan Coates

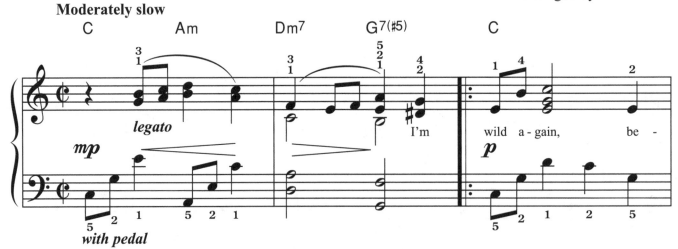

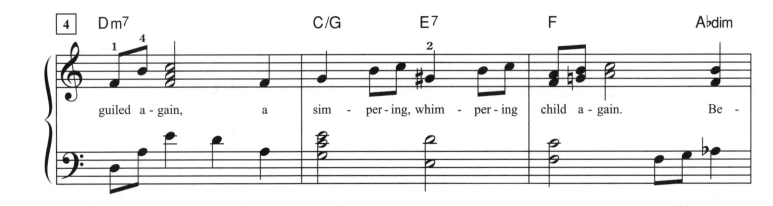

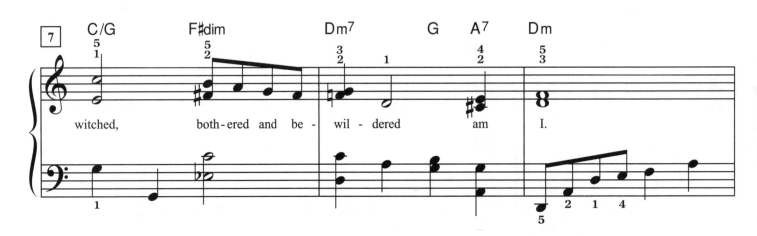

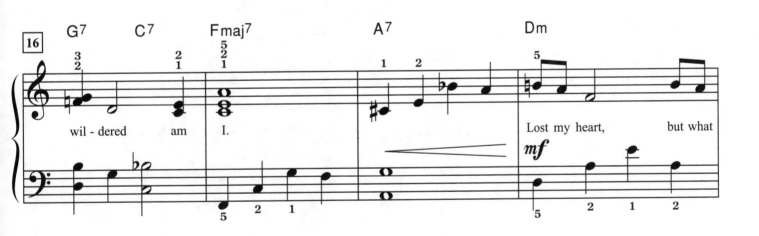

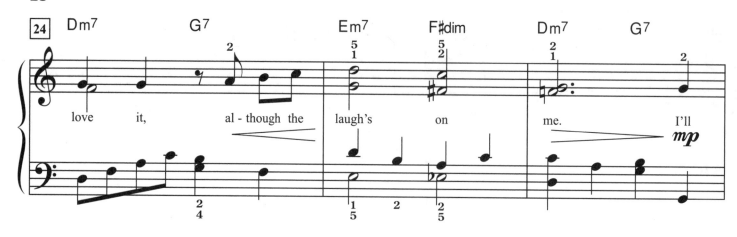

Dm7　　G7　　Em7　F#dim　Dm7　　G7

love　it,　al-though the　laugh's　on　me.　I'll

C　　Dm7　　C/G　E7

sing to him,　each　spring to him,　and　long　for the day　when I'll

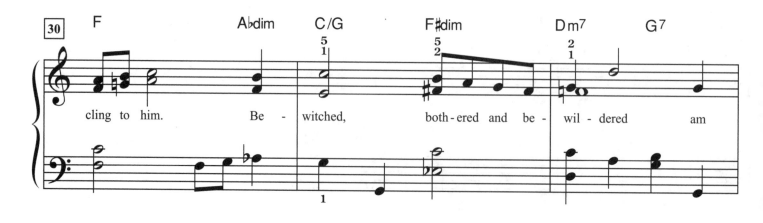

F　　A♭dim　C/G　F#dim　Dm7　　G7

cling to him.　Be-witched,　both-ered and be-wil-dered　am

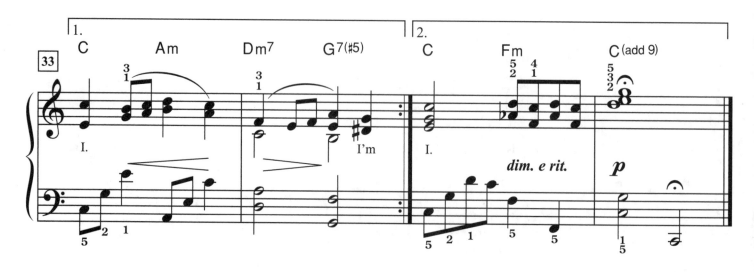

1.
C　Am　Dm7　G7(#5)

2.
C　Fm　C(add 9)

I.　I'm　I.　dim. e rit.　p

COME RAIN OR COME SHINE

"Come Rain or Come Shine" was written for the musical *St. Louis Woman* (1946). The show was based on the novel *God Sends Sunday* by African-American writer Arna Bontemps. The song has become a popular standard and has been recorded by a diverse array of artists including Frank Sinatra, Bill Evans, Judy Garland, Bette Midler, and many others.

Lyrics by Johnny Mercer
Music by Harold Arlen
Arranged by Dan Coates

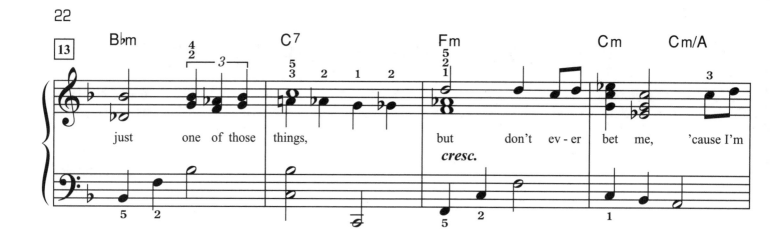

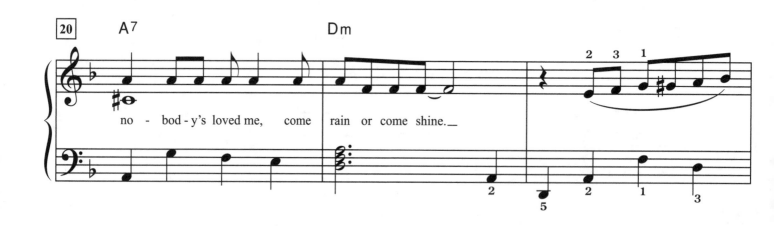

BLUES IN THE NIGHT

"Blues in the Night" was written for the 1941 dramatic film of the same name. It was sung in the movie by William Gillespie and was nominated for an Academy Award. Since then, the song has become a pop standard. Several big band artists made popular recordings of it including Cab Calloway, Woody Herman, Artie Shaw, and Dinah Shore. Additionally, there have been many contemporary artists that have recorded it: Chicago, Quincy Jones, Van Morrison, and others.

Words by Johnny Mercer
Music by Harold Arlen
Arranged by Dan Coates

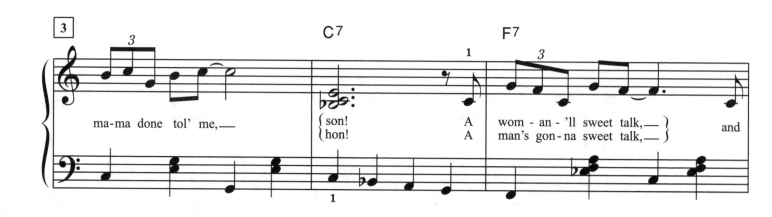

wom - an's a two - face, ___ }
man is a two - face, ___ } a wor - ri - some thing who'll leave ya t' sing the

blues ___ in the night. Now the rain's a - fall - in',

hear the train a - call - in', whoo - ee. (My ma - ma done tol' me. ___)

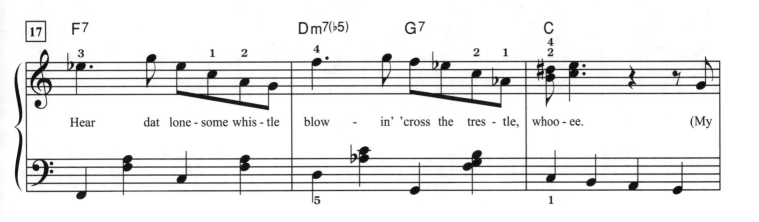

Hear dat lone - some whis - tle blow - in' 'cross the tres - tle, whoo - ee. (My

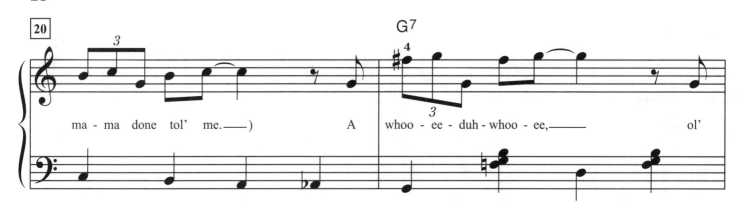

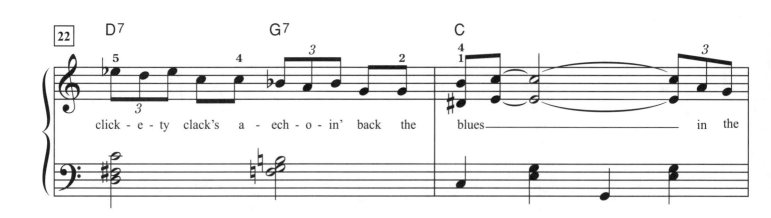

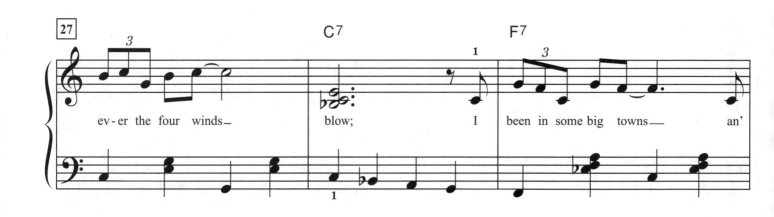

CHATTANOOGA CHOO CHOO

"Chattanooga Choo Choo" was featured in the 1941 film *Sun Valley Serenade* which starred Sonja Henie, John Payne, and Milton Berle. The film was one of only two that featured Glenn Miller and his orchestra (the other film being *Orchestra Wives*, 1942). It also featured other famous songs by Miller including "In the Mood" and "It Happened in Sun Valley." Mack Gordon and Harry Warren wrote "Chattanooga Choo Choo" while traveling on Southern Railway's "Birmingham Special" train. After 1880, most trains bound for the South from northern cities like New York had to pass through Chattanooga, Tennessee.

Music by Harry Warren
Lyrics by Mack Gordon
Arranged by Dan Coates

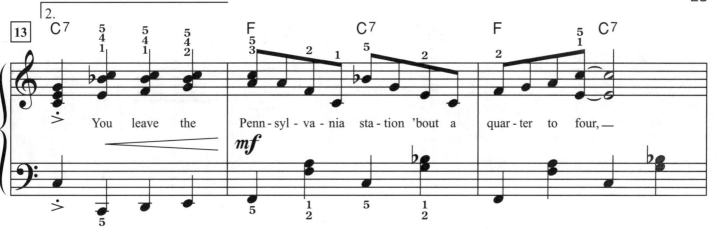

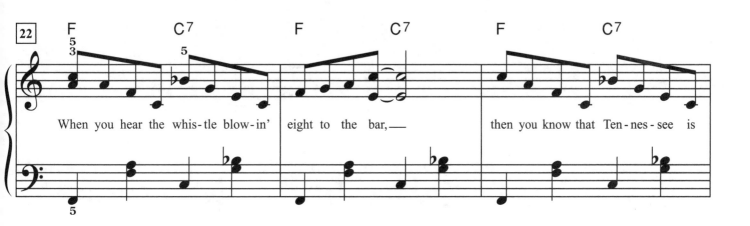

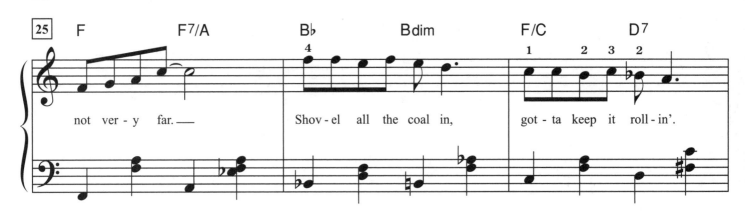

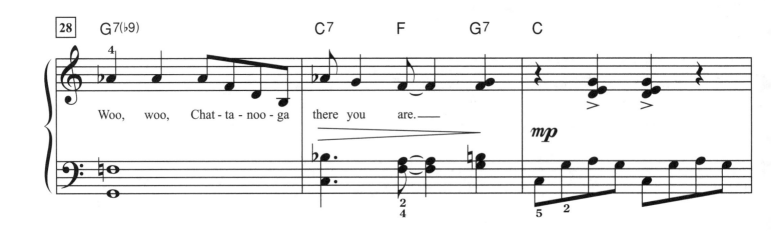

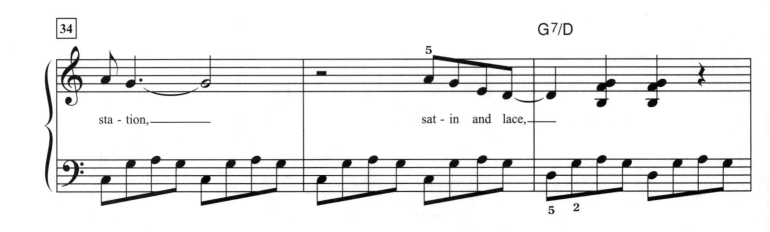

DIAMONDS ARE A GIRL'S BEST FRIEND

Carol Channing introduced "Diamonds Are a Girl's Best Friend" in the 1949 Broadway musical production of *Gentlemen Prefer Blondes*. The musical was based on a comic novel of the same name written by Anita Loos. "Diamonds Are a Girl's Best Friend" was famously sung by Marilyn Monroe in the 1953 film adaptation of the musical. This iconic performance has been the inspiration for various artists, one of whom was Madonna who used a similar set and costumes for her "Material Girl" music video.

Words by Leo Robin
Music by Jule Styne
Arranged by Dan Coates

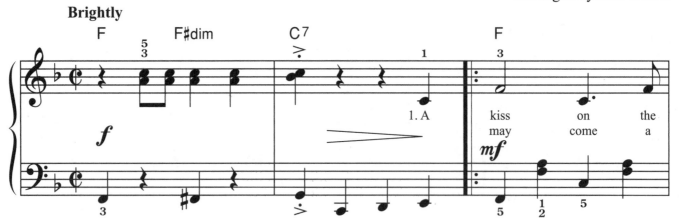

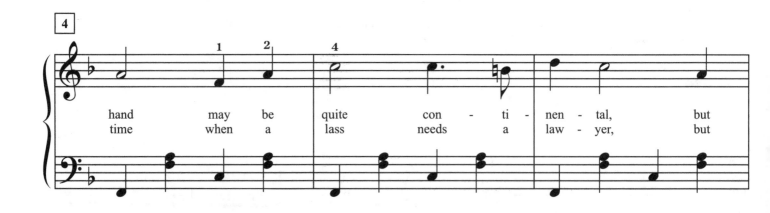

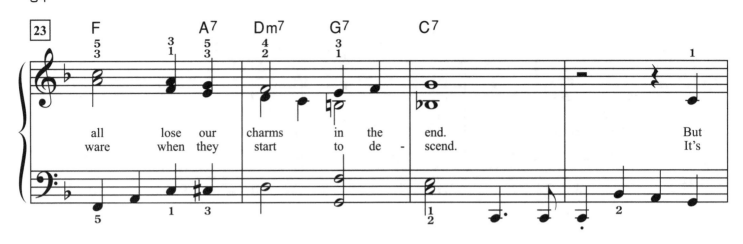

all ware lose when our they charms start in to the de- end. scend.

But It's

square- cut or pear- shaped, these rocks don't lose
then that or those lous- es go back to their

cresc.

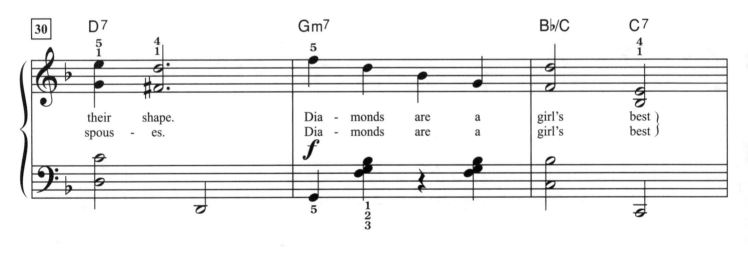

their shape.
spous- es.

Dia- monds are a girl's best ⟩
Dia- monds are a girl's best ⟩

f

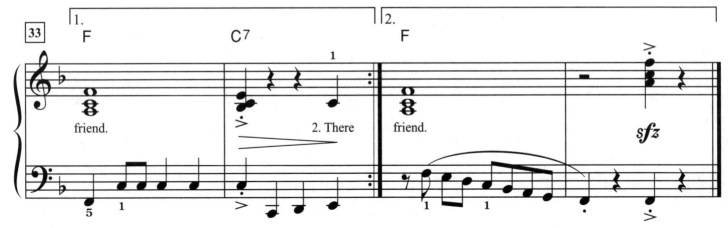

1.
friend. 2. There

2.
friend.

sfz

DON'T FENCE ME IN

In 1944, Warner Bros. released the motion picture *Hollywood Canteen*, inspired by the real life Hollywood Canteen, a club on Cahuenga Boulevard in Hollywood that provided food, dancing, and entertainment to servicemen during World War II. The club, founded by Bette Davis and John Garfield, was staffed by thousands of volunteers who served almost 3 million servicemen by the time it closed. Roy Rodgers was one of the many cameo appearances in *Hollywood Canteen*—including The Andrews Sisters, Joan Crawford, Peter Lorre, and more than 30 others—and sang "Don't Fence Me In."

Words and Music by Cole Porter
Arranged by Dan Coates

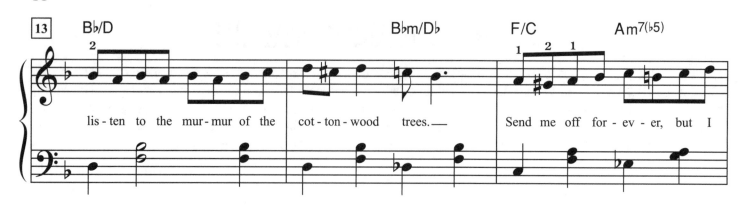

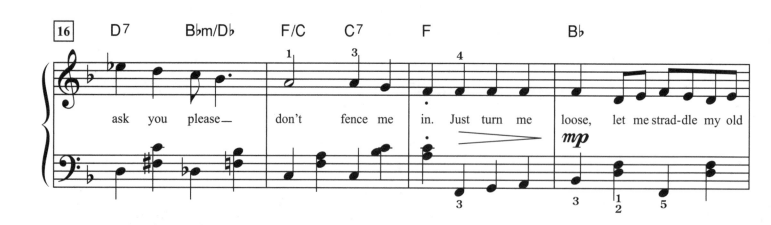

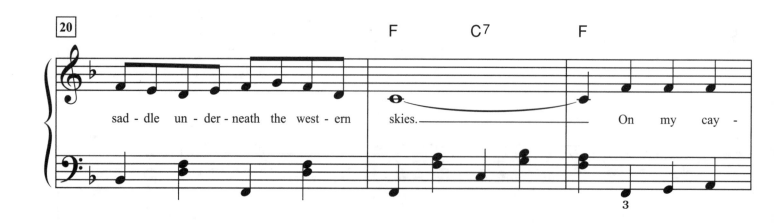

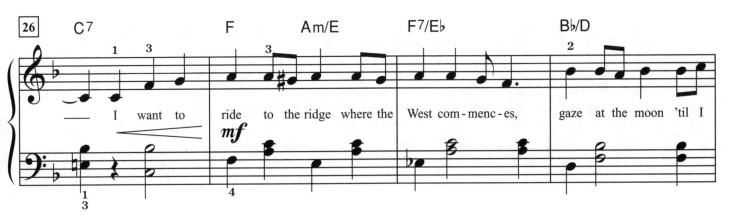

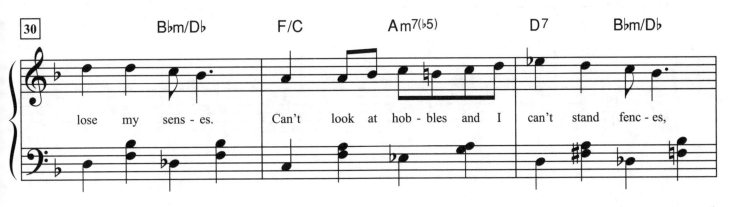

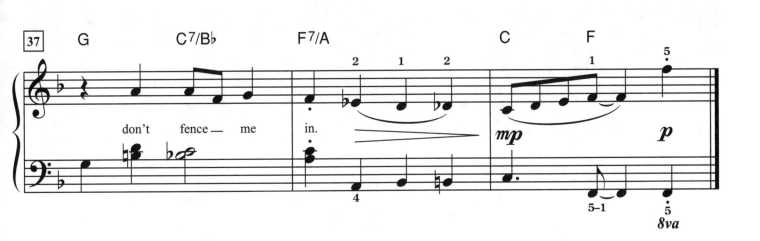

DON'T SIT UNDER THE APPLE TREE

"Don't Sit under the Apple Tree" was written for the musical film *Private Buckaroo* in 1942 and was made famous by The Andrews Sisters. The Andrews Sisters were a close-harmony singing group from Minnesota that became the best-selling female vocal group in pop music history. In addition to great success selling records, starring in Hollywood films, and making guest appearances on radio and television shows, they entertained troops regularly during World War II. "Don't Sit under the Apple Tree" is the story of a couple separated by the war.

Words and Music by
Charlie Tobias, Lew Brown and Sam H. Stept
Arranged by Dan Coates

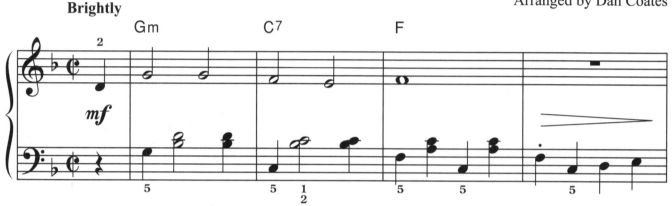

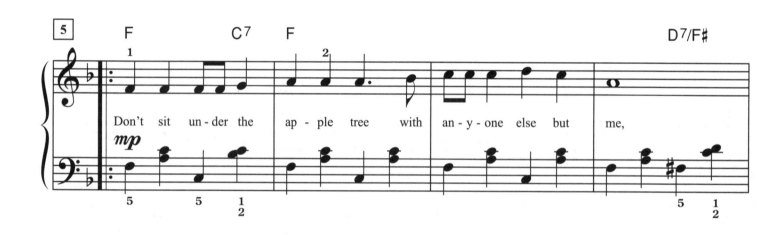

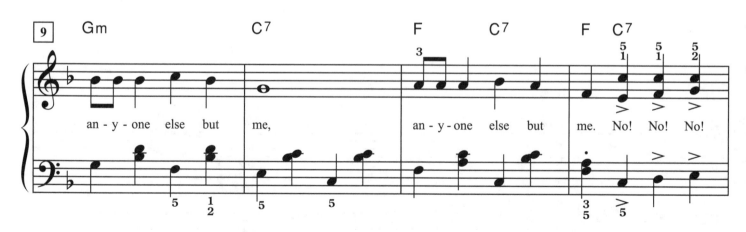

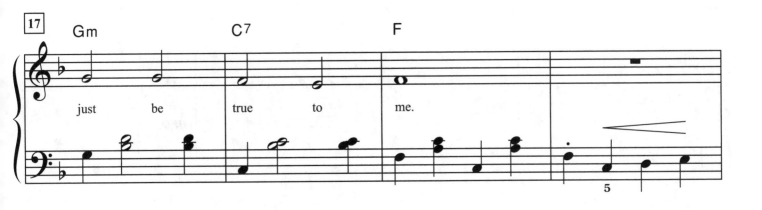

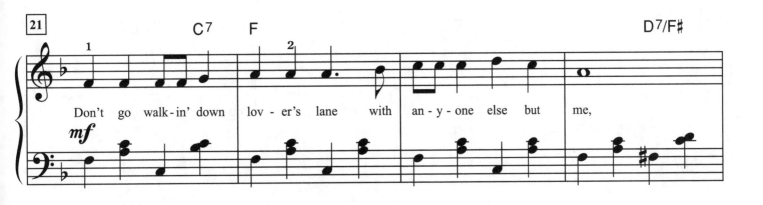

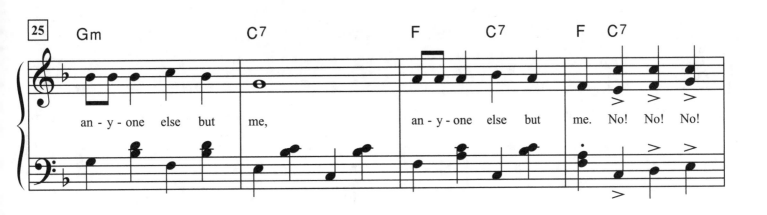

29 F   C7   F   Cm/E♭

Don't go show-ing off all your charms in some-bod-y el - se's

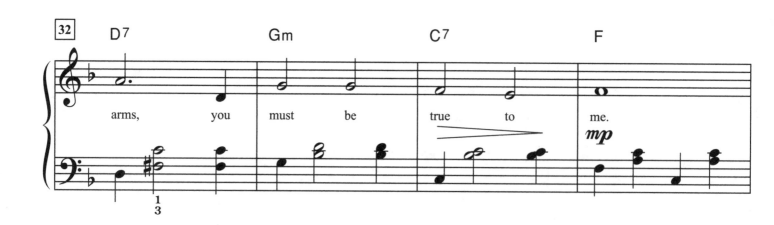

32 D7   Gm   C7   F

arms, you must be true to me.

_mp_

36 B♭   Gm7   C7

_mf_

I'm so a - fraid that the plans we made un - der -

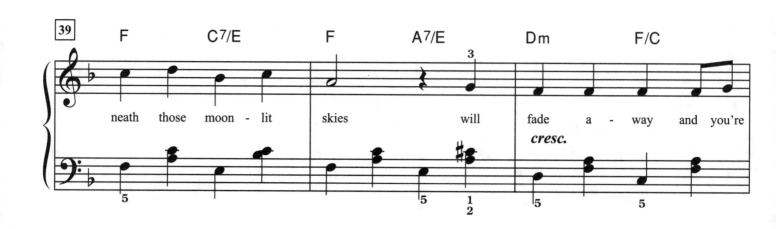

39 F   C7/E   F   A7/E   Dm   F/C

neath those moon - lit skies will fade a - way and you're

cresc.

EV'RY TIME WE SAY GOODBYE

"Ev'ry Time We Say Goodbye" was written by Cole Porter for Billy Rose's musical revue *Seven Lively Arts*. The show turned out to be a flop, but the song has become a standard. Rose was an American impresario and lyricist. He is well-known for co-writing the songs "Me and My Shadow" and "It's Only a Paper Moon."

Words and Music by Cole Porter
Arranged by Dan Coates

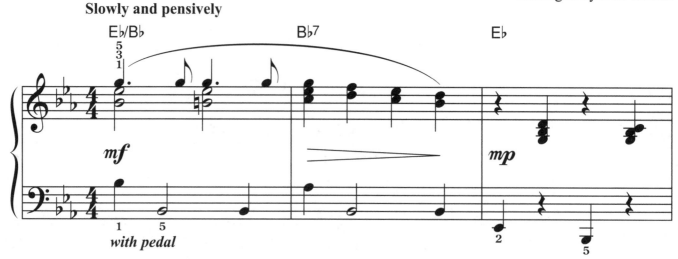

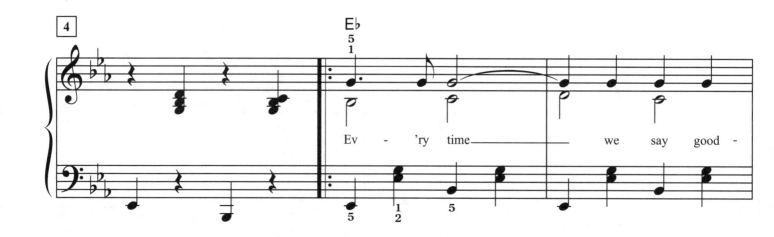

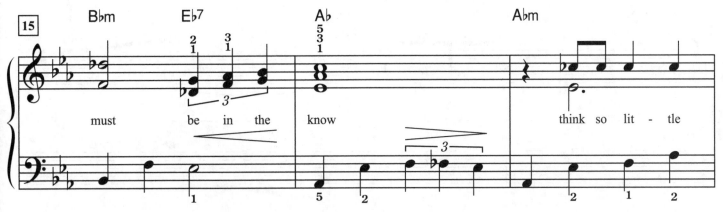

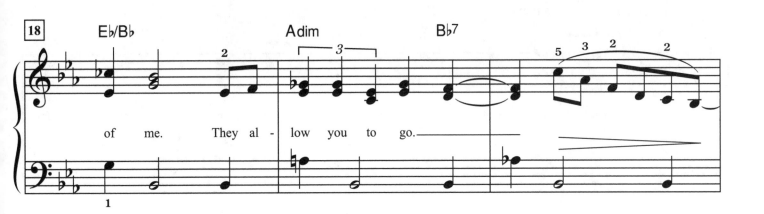

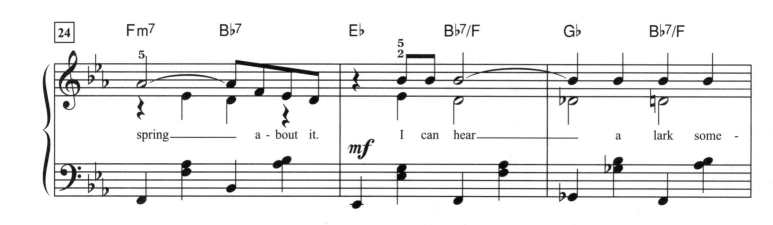

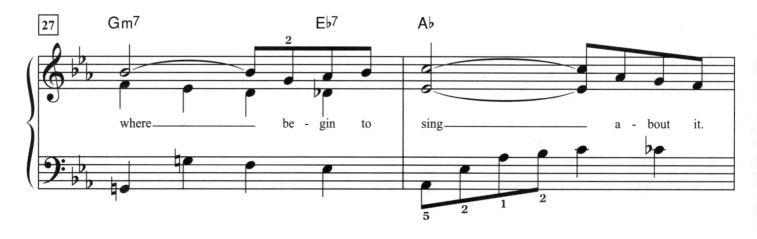

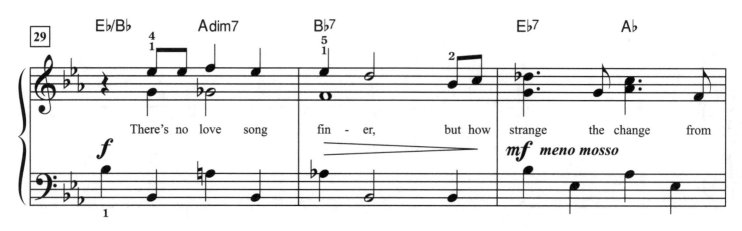

DON'T GET AROUND MUCH ANYMORE

"Don't Get Around Much Anymore" was originally titled "Never No Lament" and was first recorded as an instrumental version by Duke Ellington and his big band orchestra in 1940. Bob Russell added lyrics in 1942 and the title was changed. The song reached #1 on the R & B charts in 1943. Ellington and his orchestra toured the United States and Europe extensively before and after World War II. Ellington led this orchestra for over 50 years.

Music by Duke Ellington
Lyrics by Bob Russell
Arranged by Dan Coates

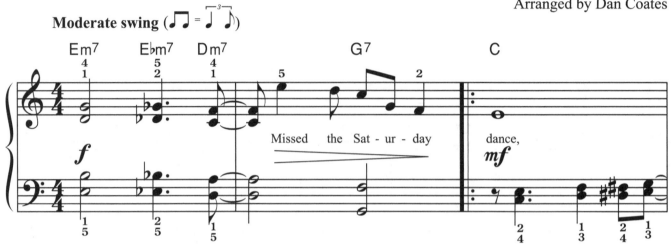

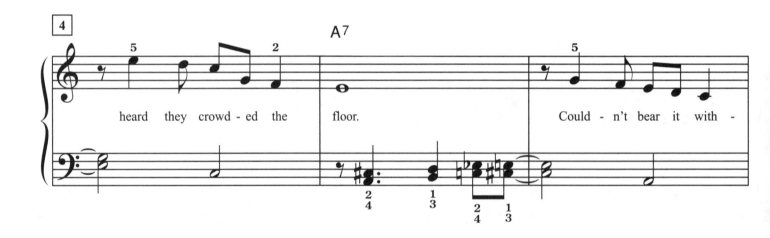

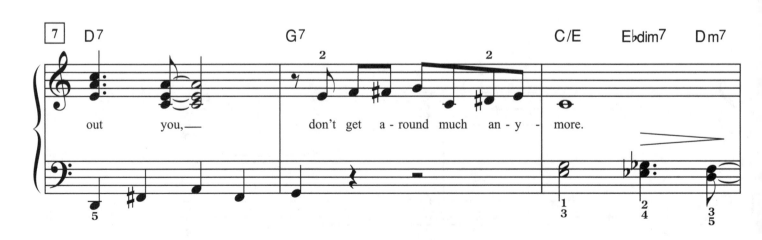

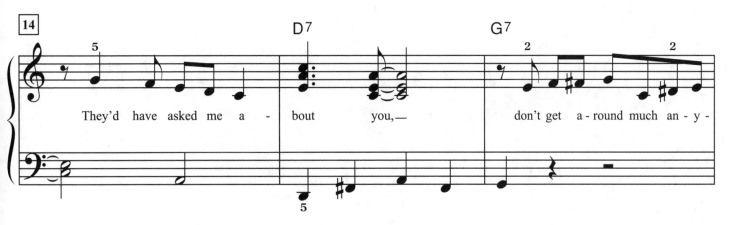

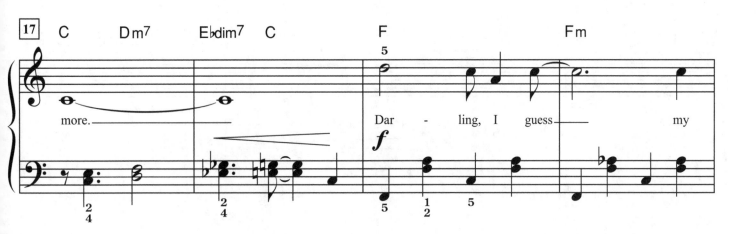

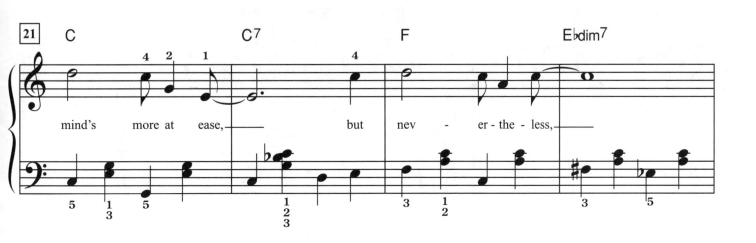

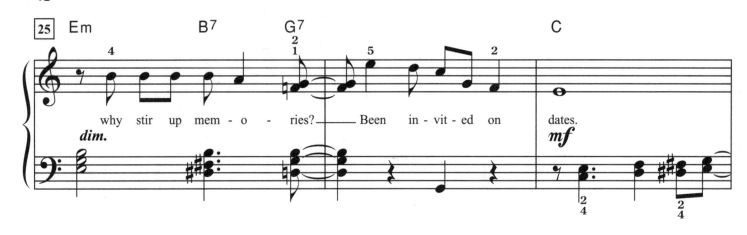

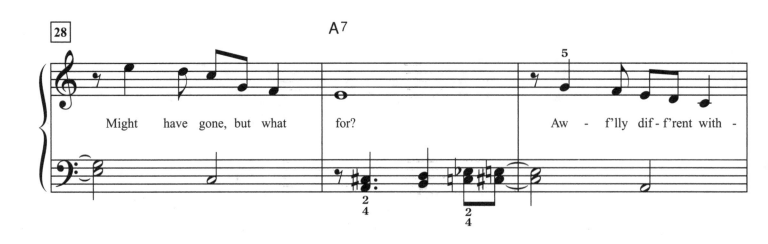

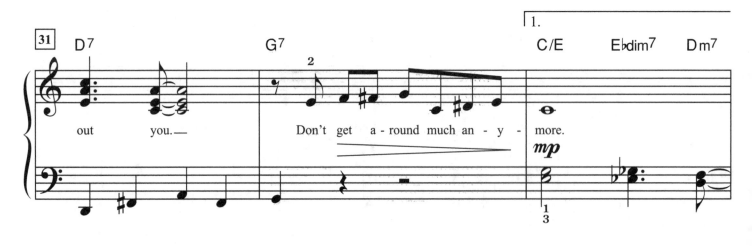

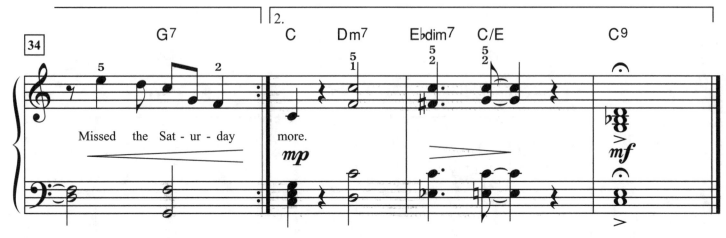

FOOLS RUSH IN

"Fool Rush In" was written by Johnny Mercer and Rube Bloom in 1940. Bloom was a Jewish American songwriter who was also a pianist, arranger, band leader, recording artist and writer. Mercer is most often remembered as a lyricist, although he was also a popular singer who recorded his own songs. Mercer and Bloom also collaborated on "Day In, Day Out."

Words by Johnny Mercer
Music by Rube Bloom
Arranged by Dan Coates

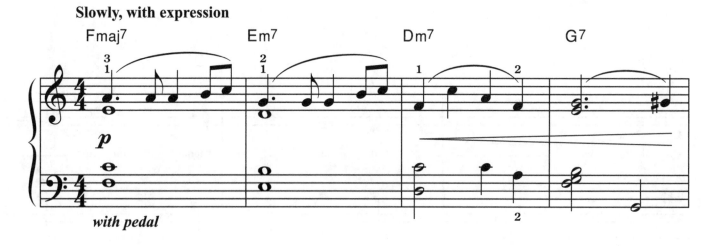

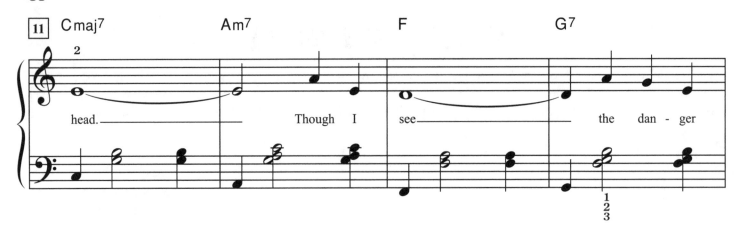

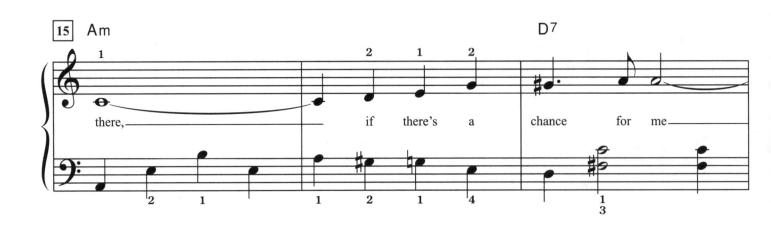

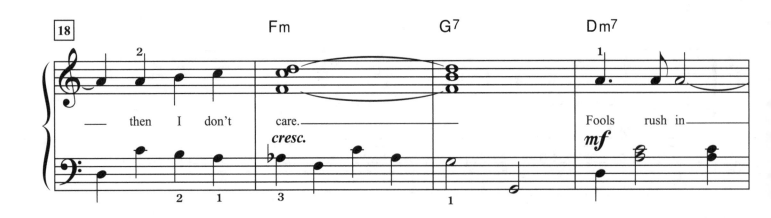

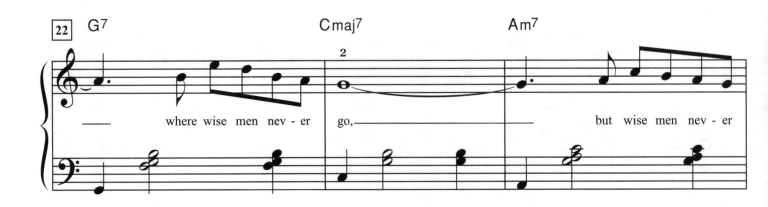

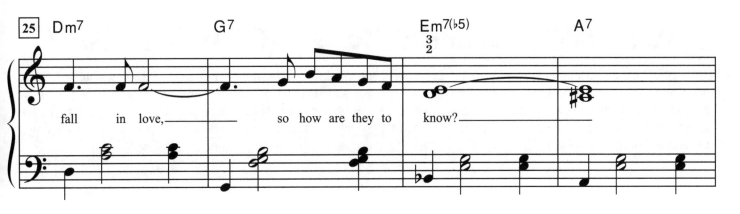

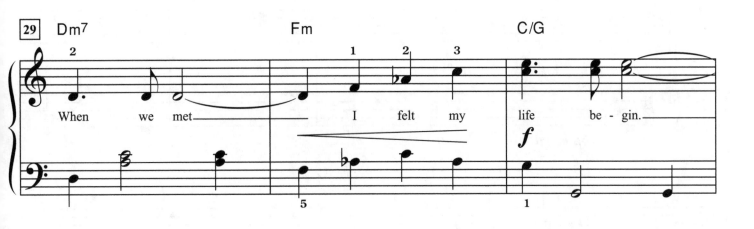

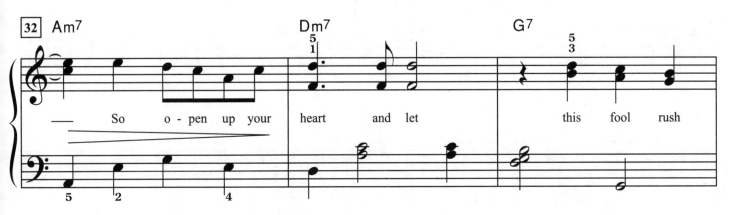

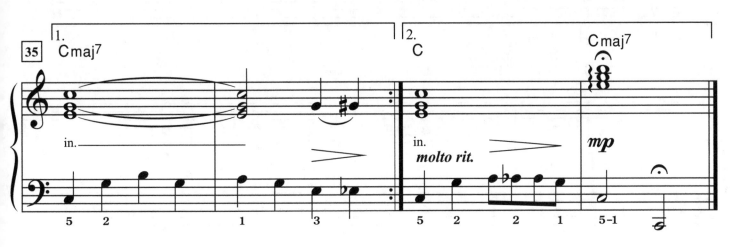

HOW ARE THINGS IN GLOCCA MORRA?

"How Are Things in Glocca Morra?" was written by Burton Lane and E. Y. Harburg for the musical *Finian's Rainbow* (1947). The show tells the tale of Irishman Finian McLongergan, who leaves his homeland with his daughter Sharon to find Rainbow Valley in the mythical state of Missitucky. There, near Fort Knox, he hopes to bury a pot of gold which he has stolen from a leprechaun, believing it will grow, multiply and make him a rich man. In 1968, the musical was adapted into a movie which starred Fred Astaire and Petula Clark. It was directed by a young, and then unknown, Francis Ford Coppola.

Words by E.Y. Harburg
Music by Burton Lane
Arranged by Dan Coates

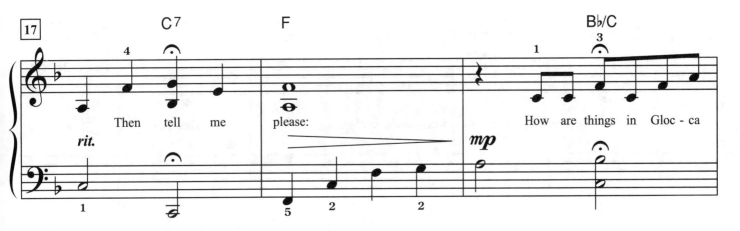

17 C7 F Bb/C

Then tell me please: How are things in Gloc - ca

Slowly, with expression

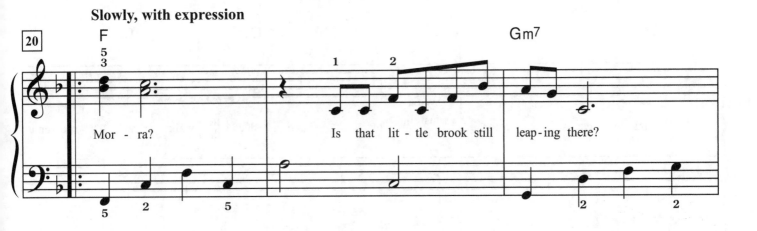

20 F Gm7

Mor - ra? Is that lit - tle brook still leap-ing there?

23 C7 Gm7 C7

Does it still run down to Don - ny - cove, through Kil - ly - begs, Kil -

26 F Bb F/A Gm F Bb/C F

ker - ry and Kil - dare? How are things in Gloc - ca Mor - ra?

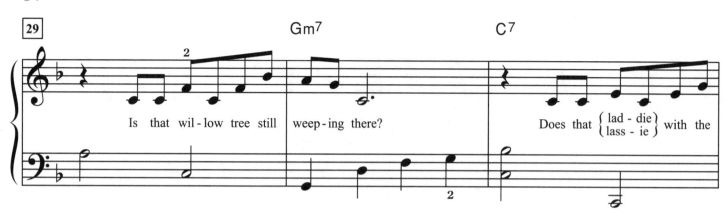

Is that wil-low tree still weep-ing there? Does that { lad - die / lass - ie } with the

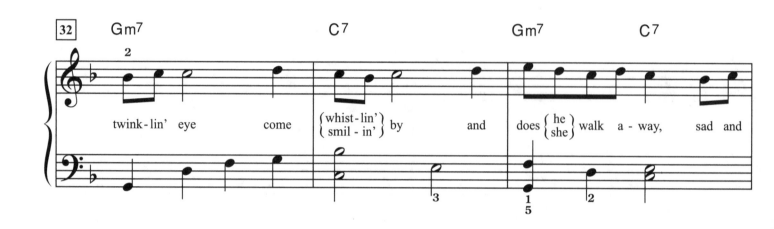

twink-lin' eye come { whist-lin' / smil-in' } by and does { he / she } walk a - way, sad and

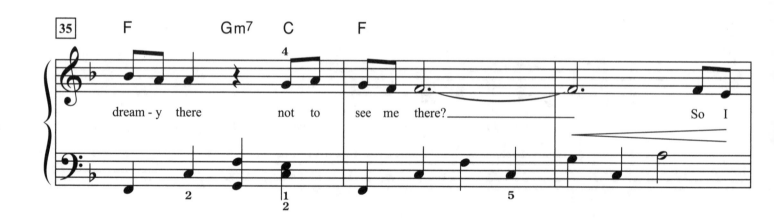

dream - y there not to see me there?_____ So I

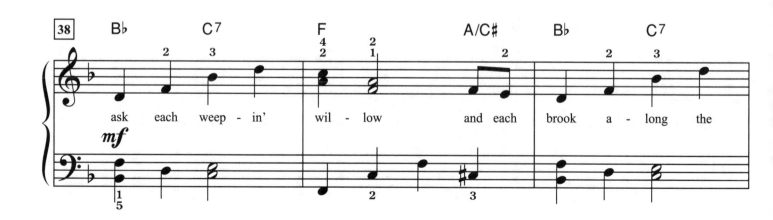

ask each weep - in' wil - low and each brook a - long the

41 F   A/C#   B♭   C7

way,   and each { lad that comes a - whist - lin' } too - ra -
                { lass that comes a - sigh - in' }

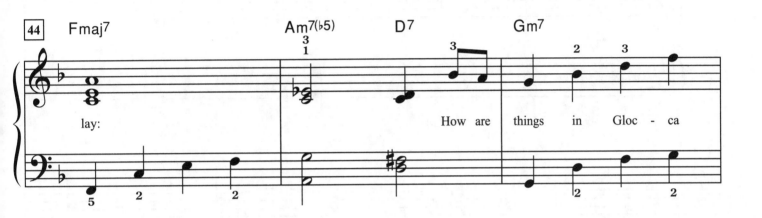

44 Fmaj7   Am7(♭5)   D7   Gm7

lay: How are things in Gloc - ca

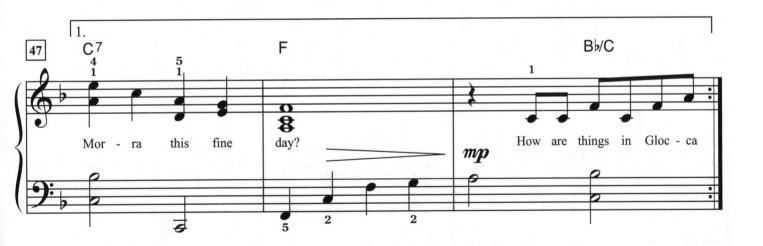

1.

47 C7   F   B♭/C

Mor - ra this fine day?   *mp*   How are things in Gloc - ca

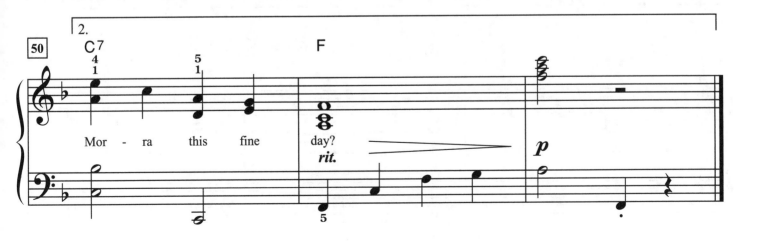

2.

50 C7   F

Mor - ra this fine day?   *rit.*   *p*

HOW HIGH THE MOON

"How High the Moon" originated in the musical *Two for the Show* which ran for 124 performances at the Booth Theatre in New York from February through May, 1940. Since then, it has become one of the most performed jazz standards. Its most famous recording was made in 1951 by the husband and wife duo Les Paul and Mary Ford which spent 25 weeks on the Billboard charts and nine weeks at #1.

Lyrics by Nancy Hamilton
Music by Morgan Lewis
Arranged by Dan Coates

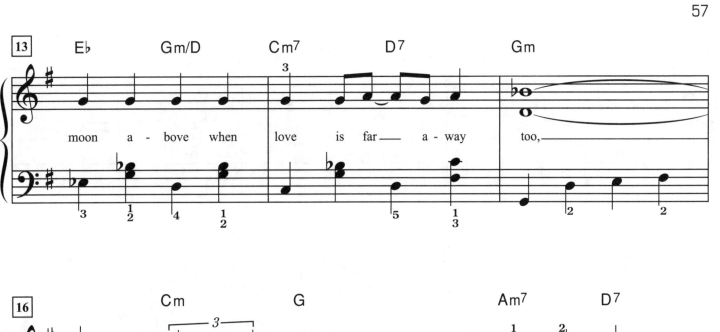

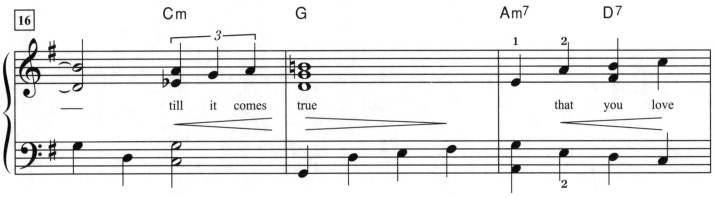

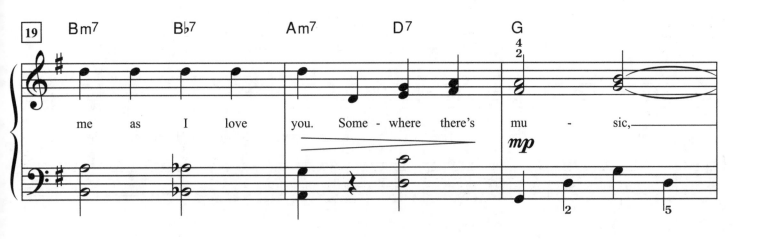

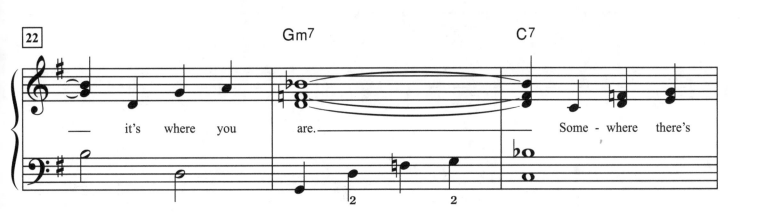

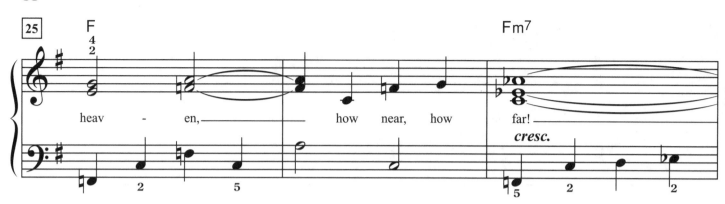

heav - en, _____ how near, how far! _____

cresc.

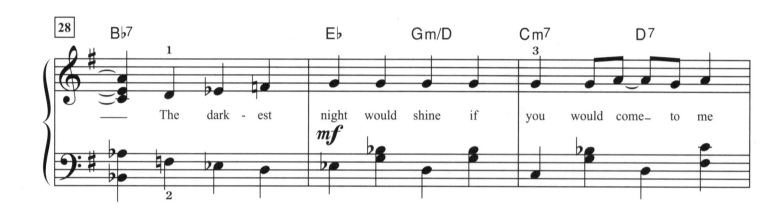

____ The dark - est night would shine if you would come _ to me

mf

soon, un - til you will, how still my heart, how high the

moon. Some - where there's moon. *rit. e dim.*

mp *p*

I COULD WRITE A BOOK

"I Could Write a Book" is from the musical *Pal Joey* (1940), which is based on an epistolary novel—a novel written in the form of letters—by John O'Hara published in *The New Yorker* magazine in the late 1930s. The musical takes place in Chicago and tells the story of Joey Evans, a second rate performer who dreams of owning his own night club ("Chez Joey"). "I Could Write a Book" is sung in the first act by Joey and Linda English, a naïve chorus girl who catches his fancy. Another famous song from *Pal Joey* is "Bewitched, Bothered and Bewildered" (see p. 18).

Words by Lorenz Hart
Music by Richard Rodgers
Arranged by Dan Coates

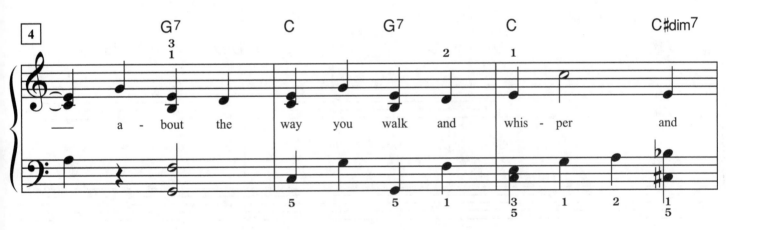

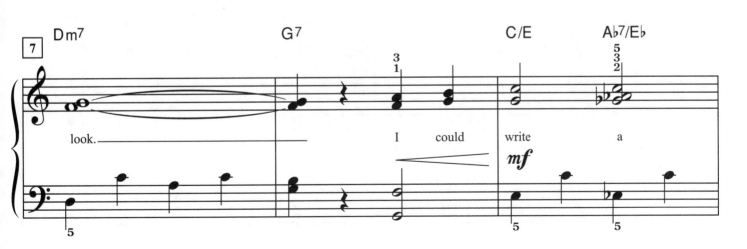

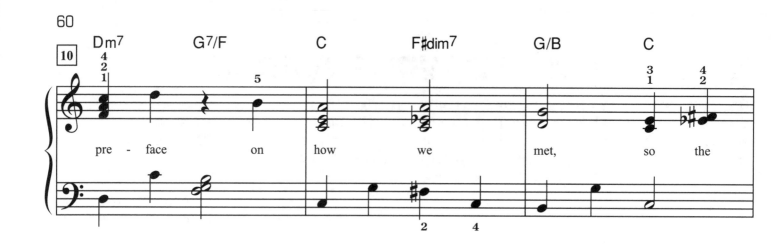

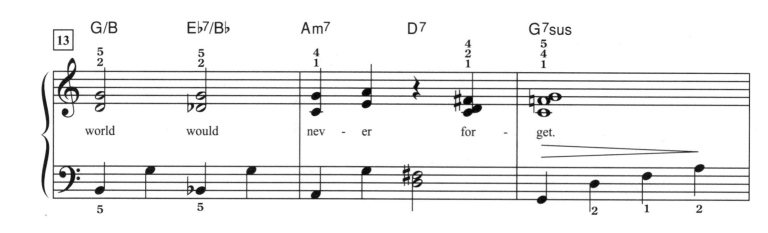

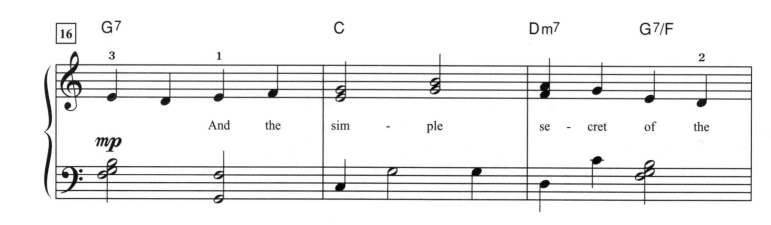

I'LL WALK ALONE

Many songs written around World War II attempted to capture the pain of separation between soldiers and their loves (see "Don't Sit under the Apple Tree" on p. 38). "I'll Walk Alone" is one of these songs and is told from the perspective of the lover who stays at home. The song was first sung by Dinah Shore in the 1944 film *Follow the Boys*, one of many feature films produced in Hollywood during the 1940s made to boost troop morale during the war.

Words and Music by
Sammy Cahn and Jule Styne
Arranged by Dan Coates

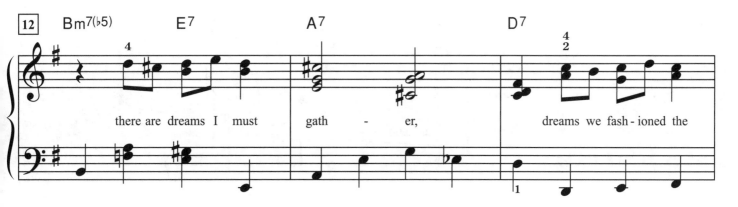

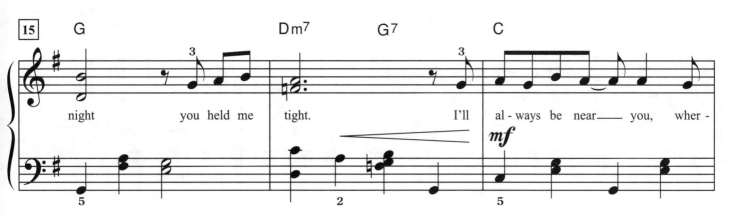

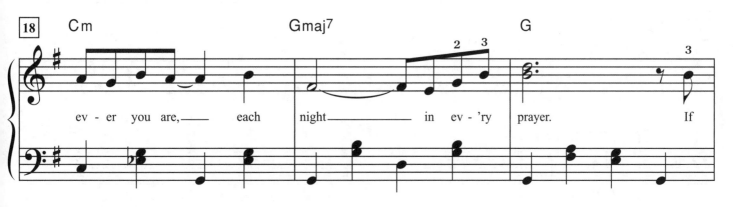

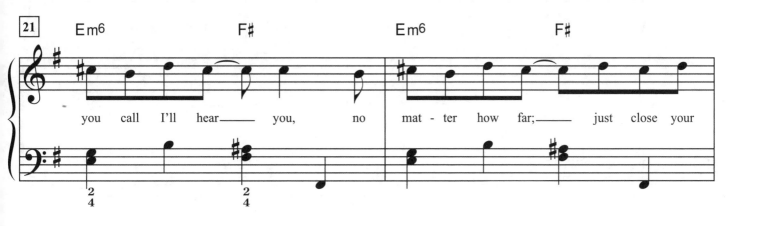

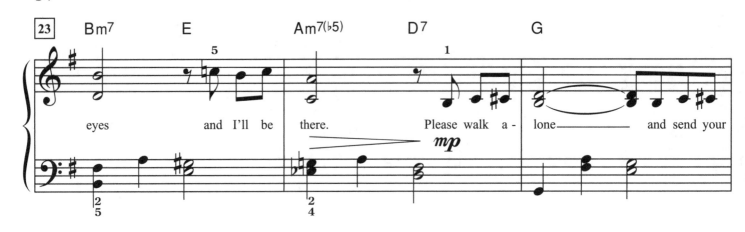

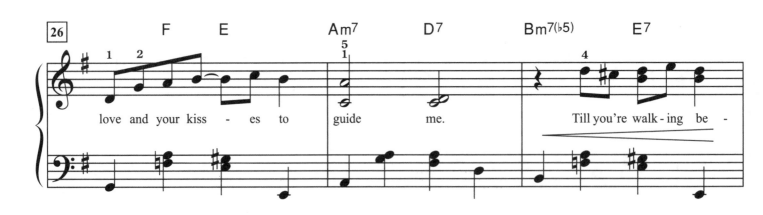

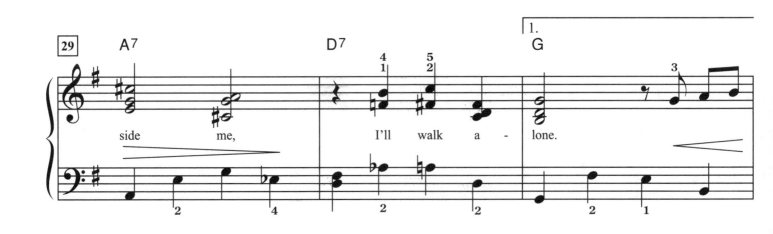

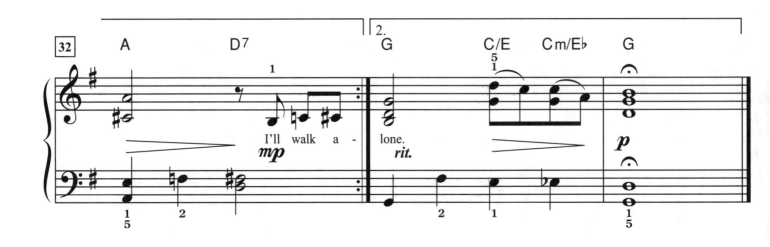

LA VIE EN ROSE

"La Vie en rose" is the signature song of French pop icon Edith Piaf. The title translates literally to "The Life in Pink." The English equivalent would be "Life Through Rose-Colored Glasses." *La Vie en rose* is also the title of two films about Piaf. The first was a 1998 documentary, and the second was a 2007 feature film. The latter starred Marion Cotillard as Edith Piaf, a performance which won the Academy Award for Best Actress. "La Vie en rose" has become a standard and has been recorded and performed by many popular artists including Bing Crosby, Placido Domingo, Donna Summer, and many others.

Original French Lyrics by Edith Piaf
English Lyrics by Mack David

Music by Luis Guglielmi
Arranged by Dan Coates

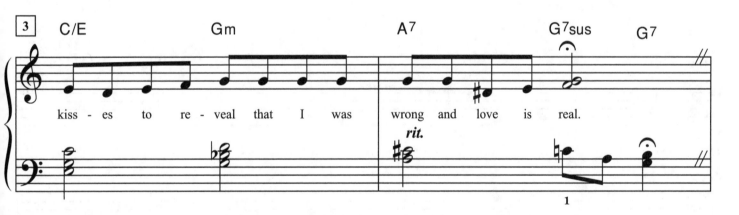

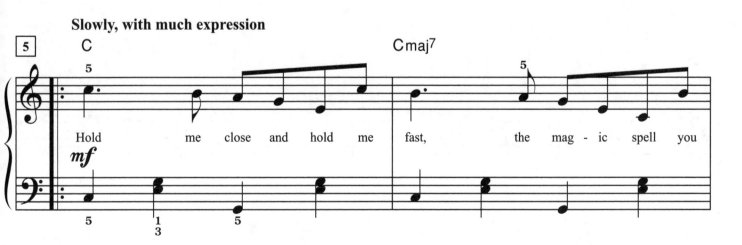

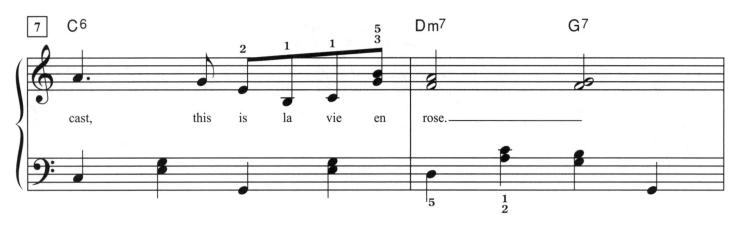

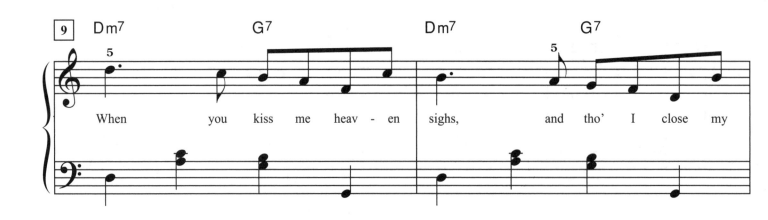

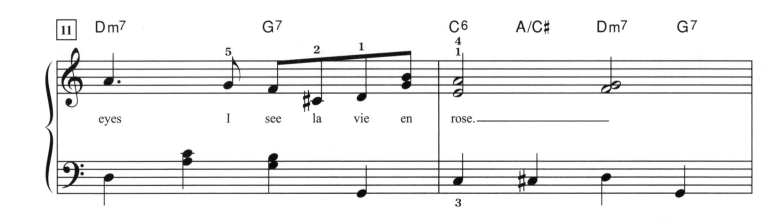

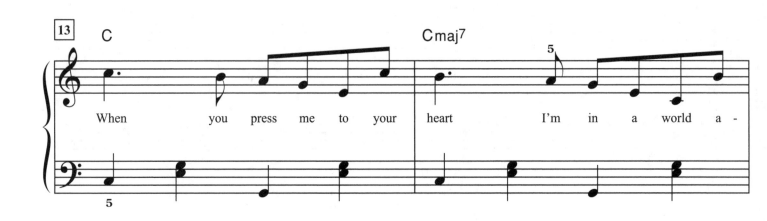

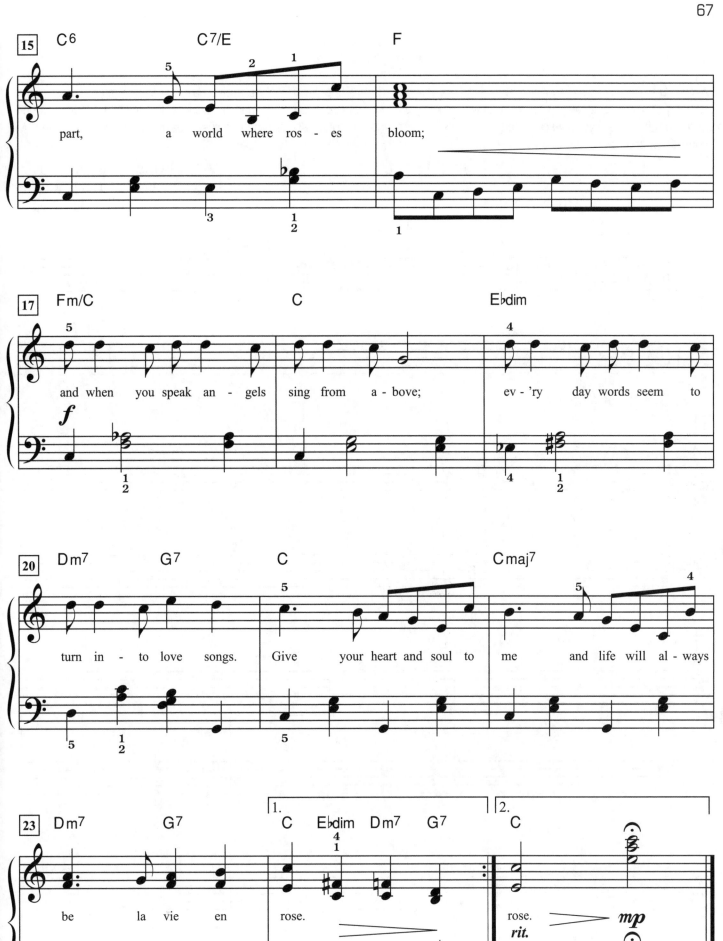

LAURA

Laura (1944) is an Academy Award-winning film noir based on a popular 1943 detective novel by Vera Caspary. The film's brooding theme music was written by David Raksin, who composed it after he had unfortunately received a "Dear John" letter from his wife. Lyrics were added by Johnny Mercer, and the song has become a jazz standard having been recorded by hundreds of artists.

Lyrics by Johnny Mercer
Music by David Raksin
Arranged by Dan Coates

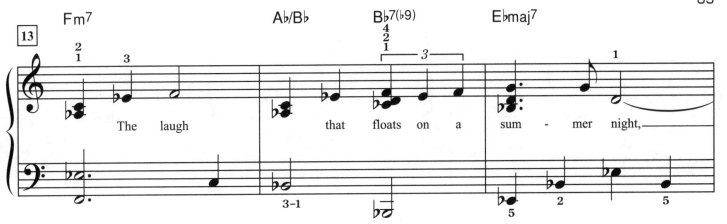

The laugh that floats on a sum - mer night,

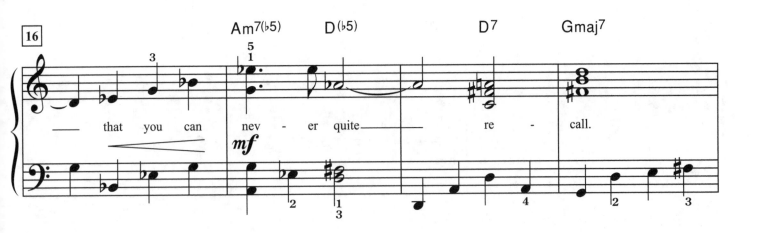

that you can nev - er quite re - call.

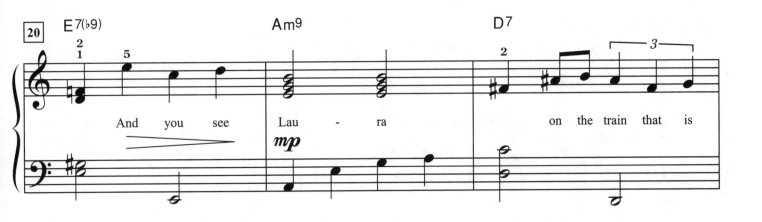

And you see Lau - ra on the train that is

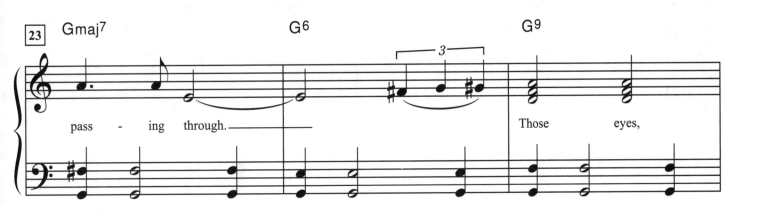

pass - ing through. Those eyes,

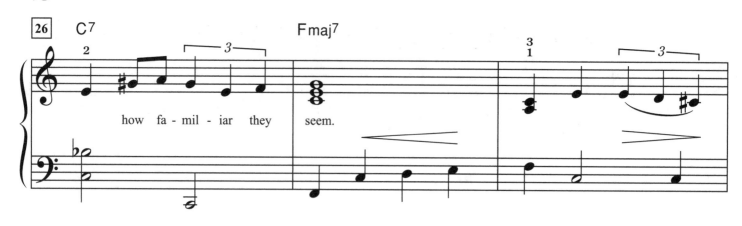

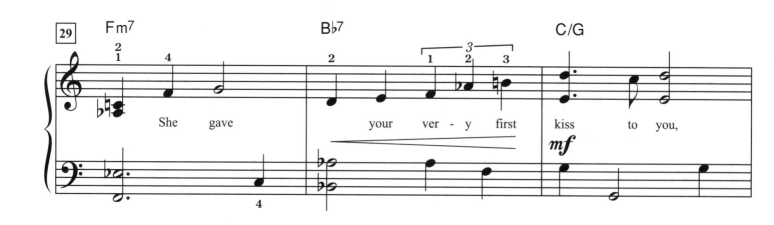

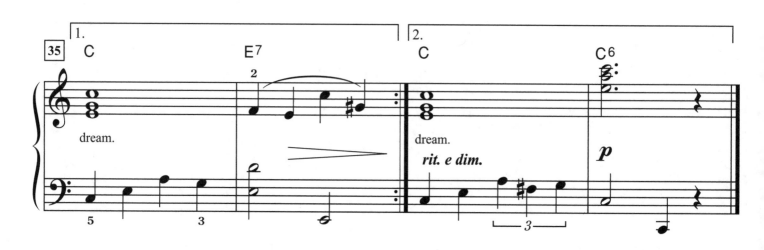

MOONLIGHT IN VERMONT

"Moonlight in Vermont" was written by John Blackburn and Karl Suessdorf in 1943. The verses of the song have the pattern five syllables, seven syllables, five syllables, making each verse a haiku. It is also worth noting that the lyrics of the song do not rhyme. "Moonlight in Vermont" is the unofficial state song of Vermont and has been recorded by Louis Armstrong, Ella Fitzgerald, Willie Nelson, Frank Sinatra, Margaret Whiting, and many others.

Music by Karl Suessdorf
Lyric by John Blackburn
Arranged by Dan Coates

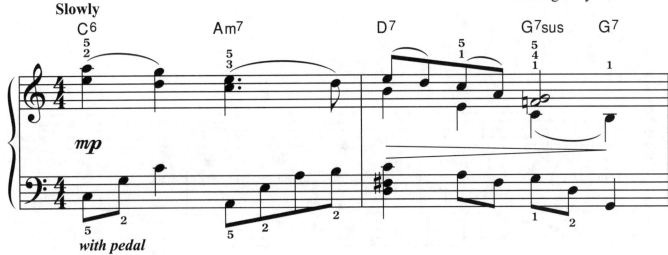

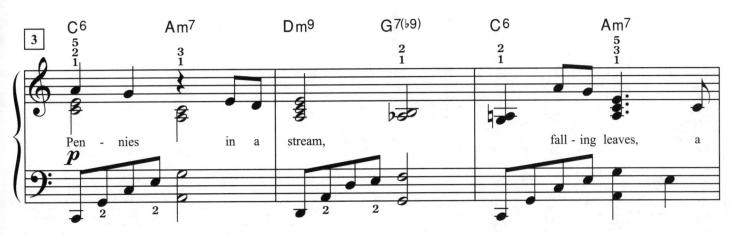

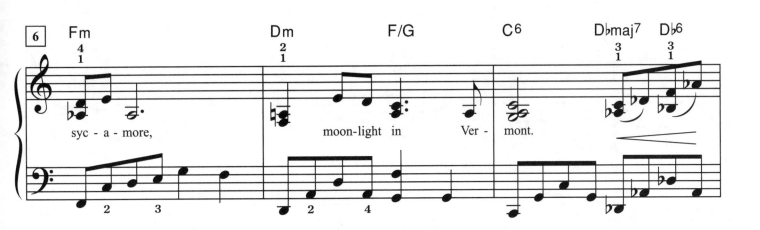

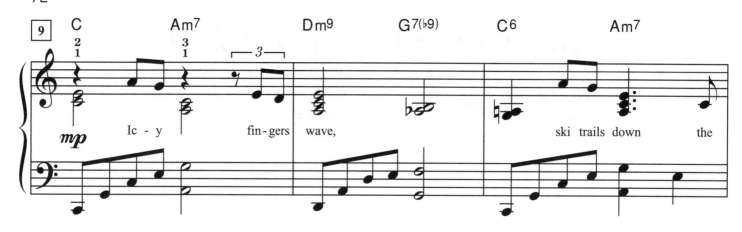

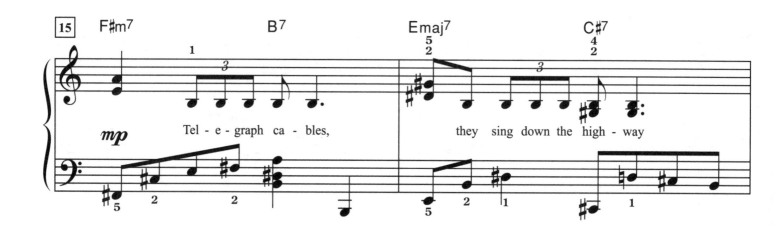

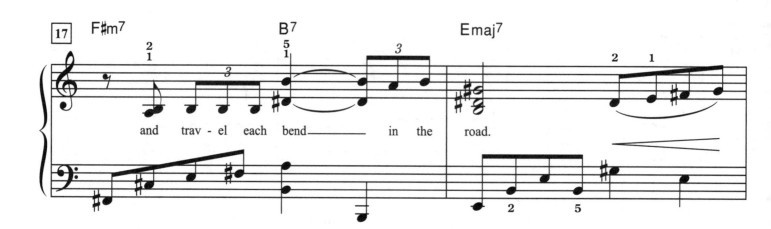

MAIRZY DOATS

"Mairzy Doats" is a novelty song which was written in 1943 by Milton Drake, Al Hoffman, and Jerry Livingston. It was based on an English nursery rhyme and was first performed on the radio by Al Trace and His Silly Symphonists. A version by The Merry Macs, a close-harmony vocal group from Minnesota, reached #1 on the pop charts.

Words and Music by
Milton Drake, Al Hoffman and Jerry Livingston
Arranged by Dan Coates

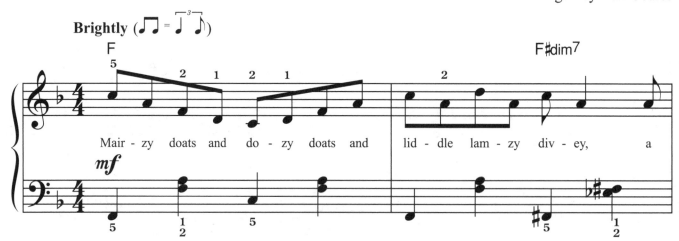

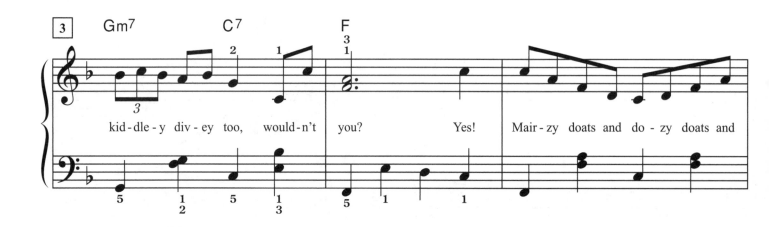

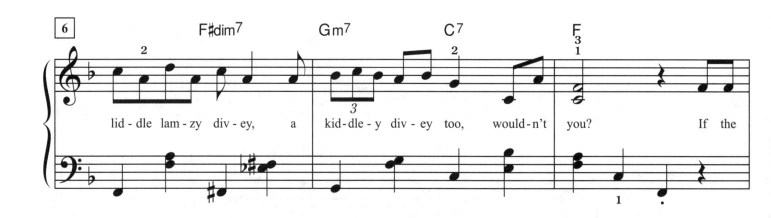

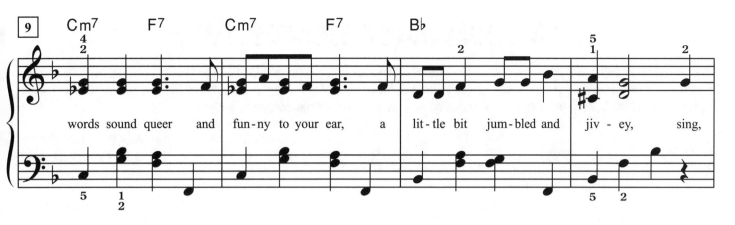

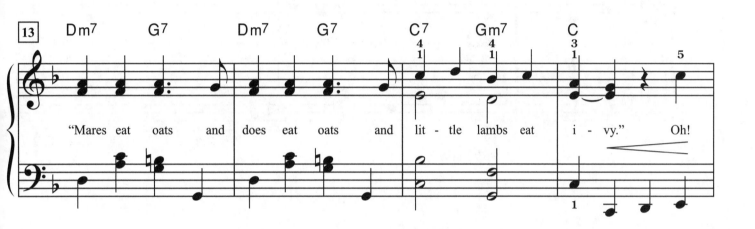

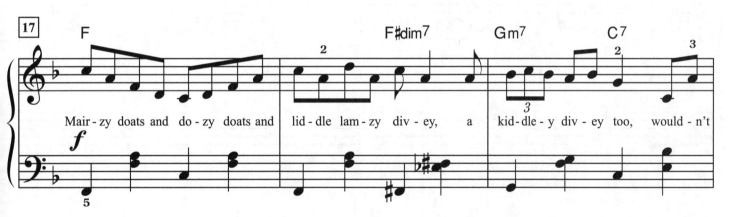

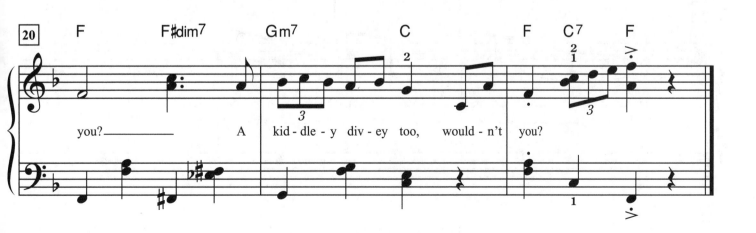

MOONLIGHT SERENADE

"Moonlight Serenade" was originally titled "Now I Lay Me Down to Weep" and released as the B-side to Glenn Miller's "Sunrise Serenade." The instrumental tune became a huge hit and Miller's signature song, capturing the big band sound of the 1940s. Lyrics were added by Mitchell Parish, and the song has been used in numerous films and on television.

Music by Glenn Miller
Lyric by Mitchell Parish
Arranged by Dan Coates

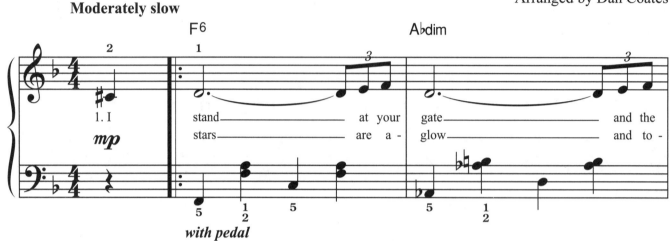

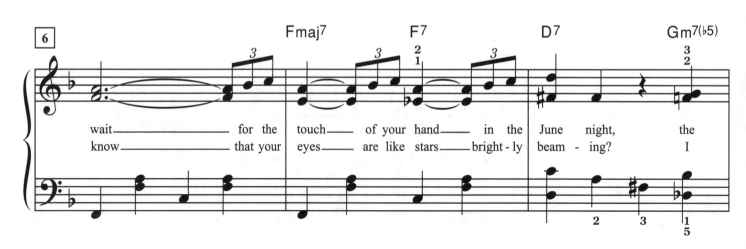

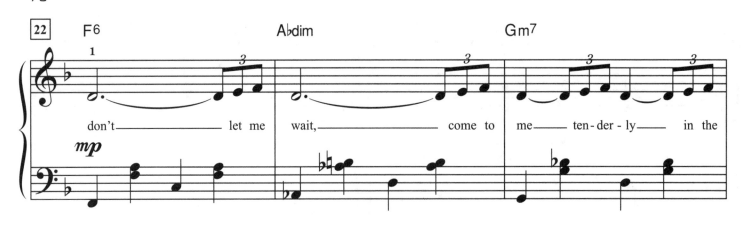

don't_____ let me wait,_____ come to me ten - der - ly____ in the

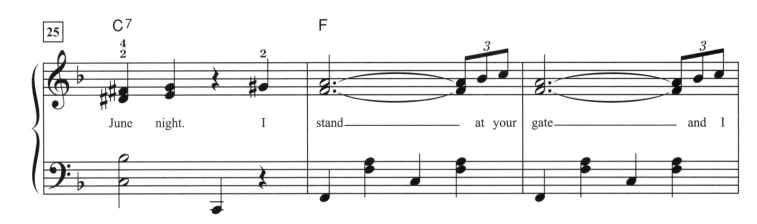

June night. I stand_____ at your gate_____ and I

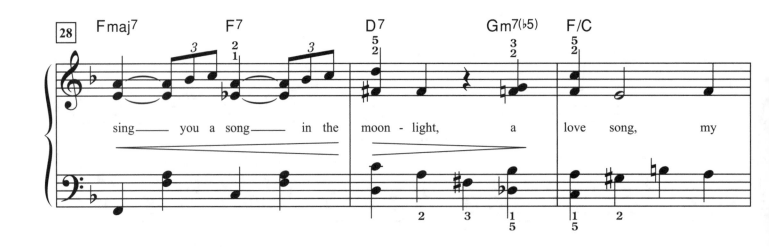

sing____ you a song____ in the moon - light, a love song, my

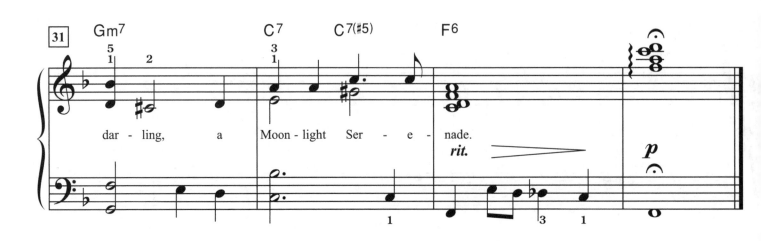

dar - ling, a Moon - light Ser - e - nade.

MY FOOLISH HEART

My Foolish Heart was an Academy Award-nominated film adapted from a short story ("Uncle Wiggily in Connecticut") by J. D. Salinger. The film was not well received by the critics, and, as a result, Salinger prevented filmmakers from producing any further movies based on his works, including the famous *Catcher in the Rye*. Despite this, the title song has become a jazz standard, having been recorded by Bill Evans, George Shearing, Mel Tormé, and many others.

Words by Ned Washington
Music by Victor Young
Arranged by Dan Coates

Slowly and expressively

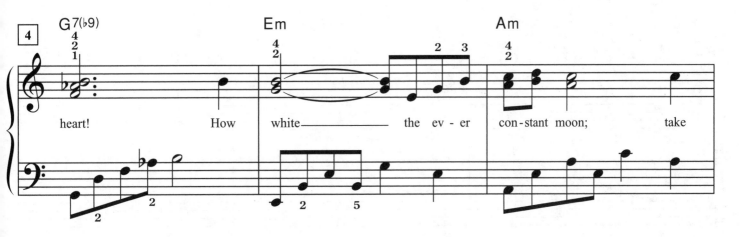

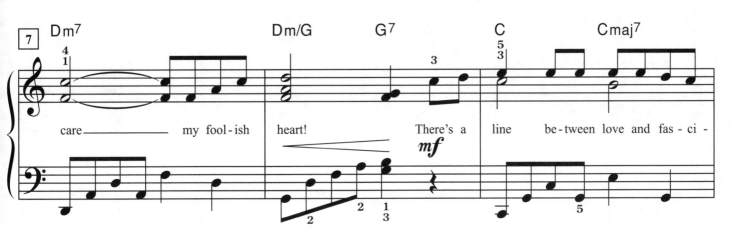

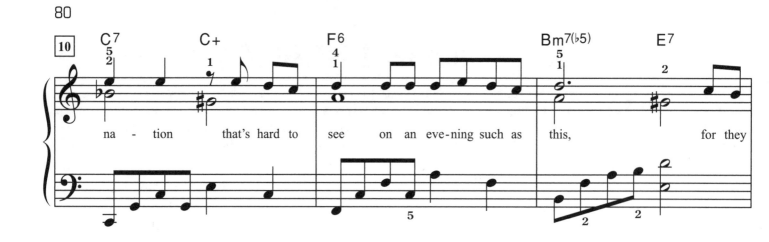

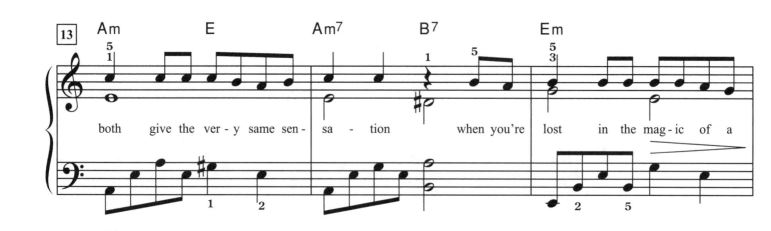

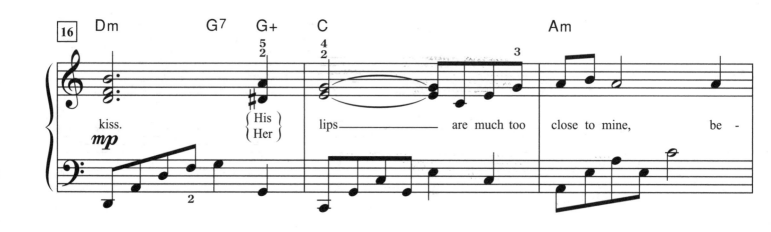

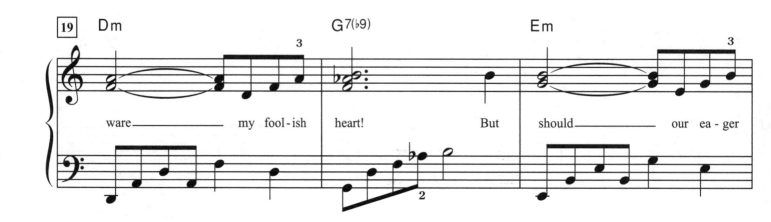

NEW YORK, NEW YORK

"New York, New York" is from the 1944 Broadway musical *On the Town* by Leonard Bernstein, Betty Comden, and Adolph Green. The musical was based on the 1944 ballet *Fancy Free* and was adapted into a film in 1949. The story is about three sailors who visit New York City on shore leave before heading off for war. They sing "New York, New York" near the beginning of the show when they first arrive in the city.

Lyrics by Betty Comden and Adolph Green
Music by Leonard Bernstein
Arranged by Dan Coates

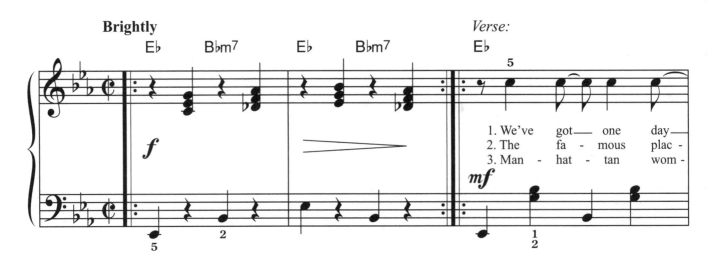

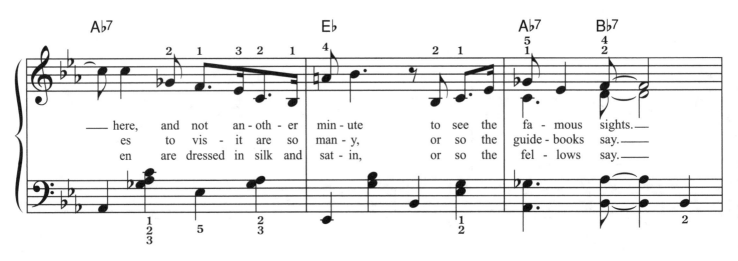

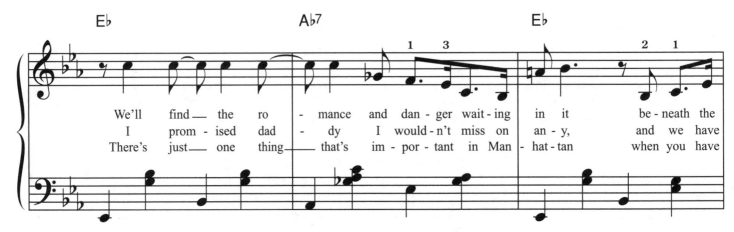

OPUS ONE

Tommy Dorsey was a famous jazz trombonist and dance band leader in the 1930s, 1940s, and 1950s. As a performer, he was known for his beautiful and lyrical ballad playing. His band was incredibly successful with well over 100 hits on the Billboard charts including "I'm Getting Sentimental Over You," "There Are Such Things," and "Opus One."

Words and Music by Sy Oliver and Sig Garris
Arranged by Dan Coates

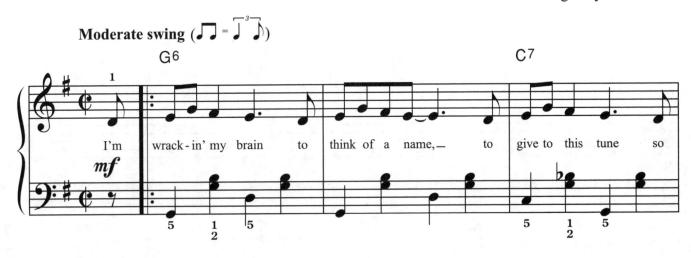

I'm wrack-in' my brain to think of a name,— to give to this tune so

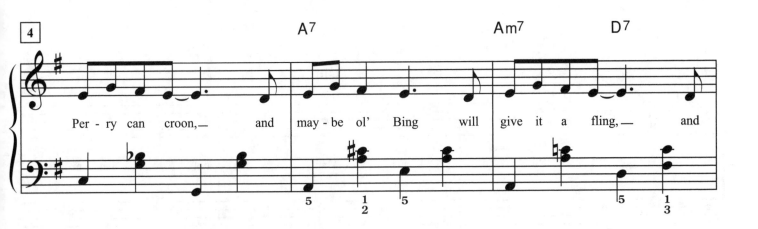

Per-ry can croon,— and may-be ol' Bing will give it a fling,— and

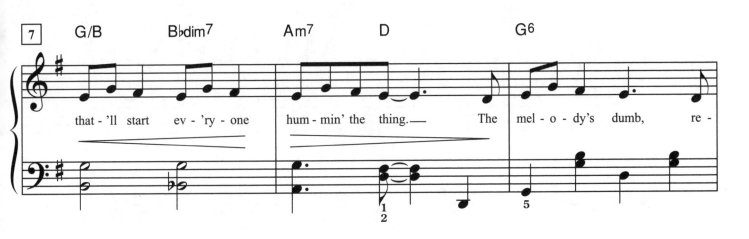

that-'ll start ev-'ry-one hum-min' the thing.— The mel-o-dy's dumb, re-

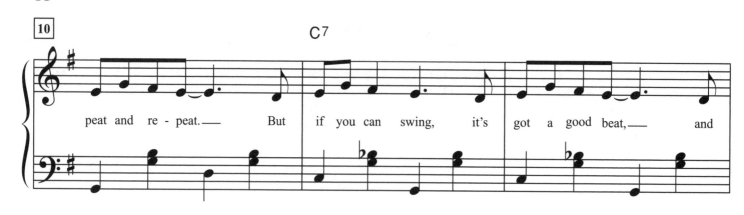

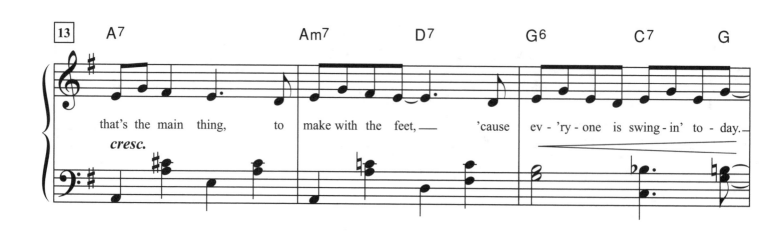

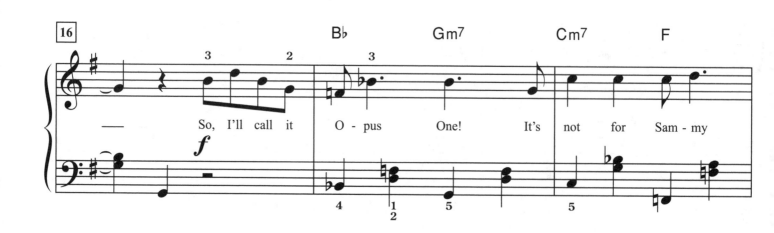

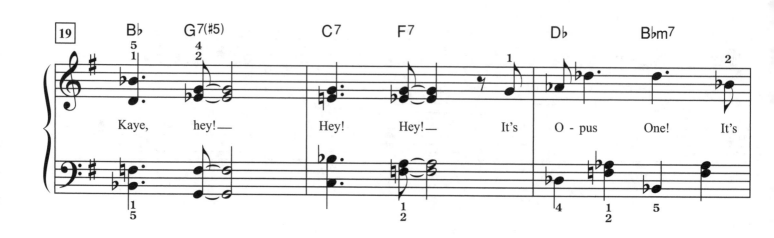

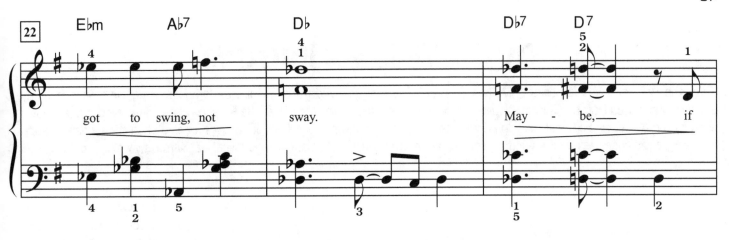

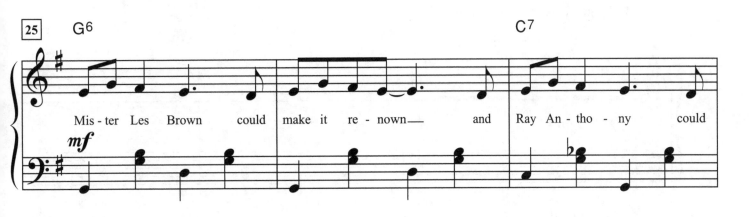

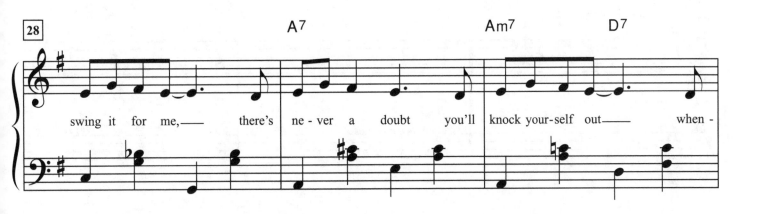

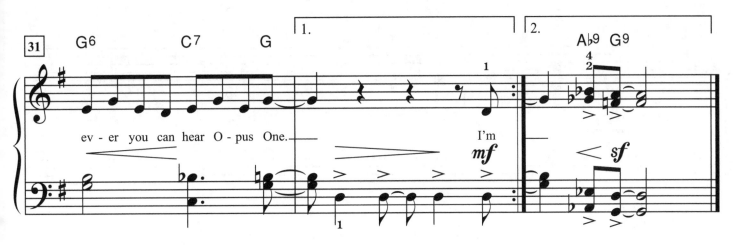

OVER THE RAINBOW

"Over the Rainbow" was featured in MGM's classic 1939 film *The Wizard of Oz*. It was famously sung in the film by Judy Garland who played Dorothy, a Kansas farm girl who yearns for a better life. "Over the Rainbow" has been voted the #1 movie song by the American Film Institute. In addition to being the signature song for Garland, it has also been the signature song for two great singers whose lives and careers ended prematurely—Eva Cassidy and Israel "Iz" Kamakawiwo'ole.

Music by Harold Arlen
Lyrics by E.Y. Harburg
Arranged by Dan Coates

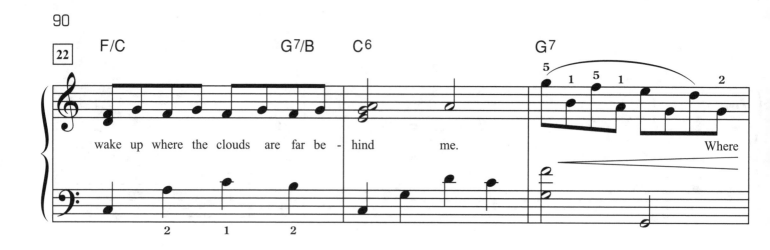

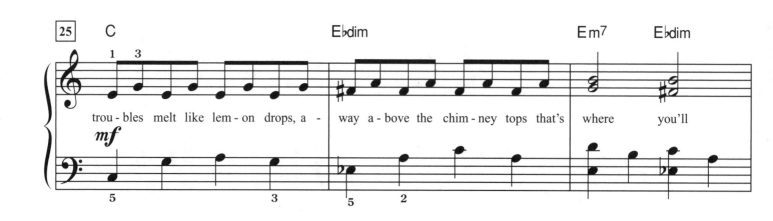

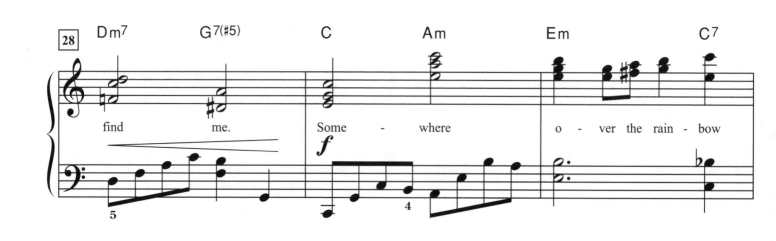

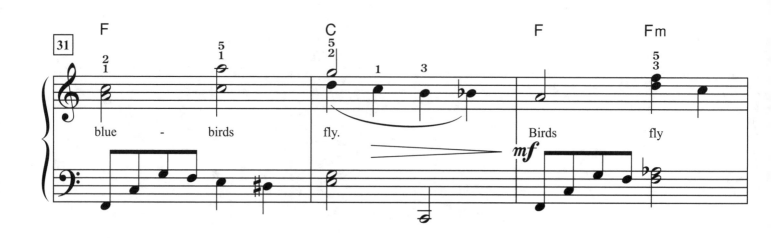

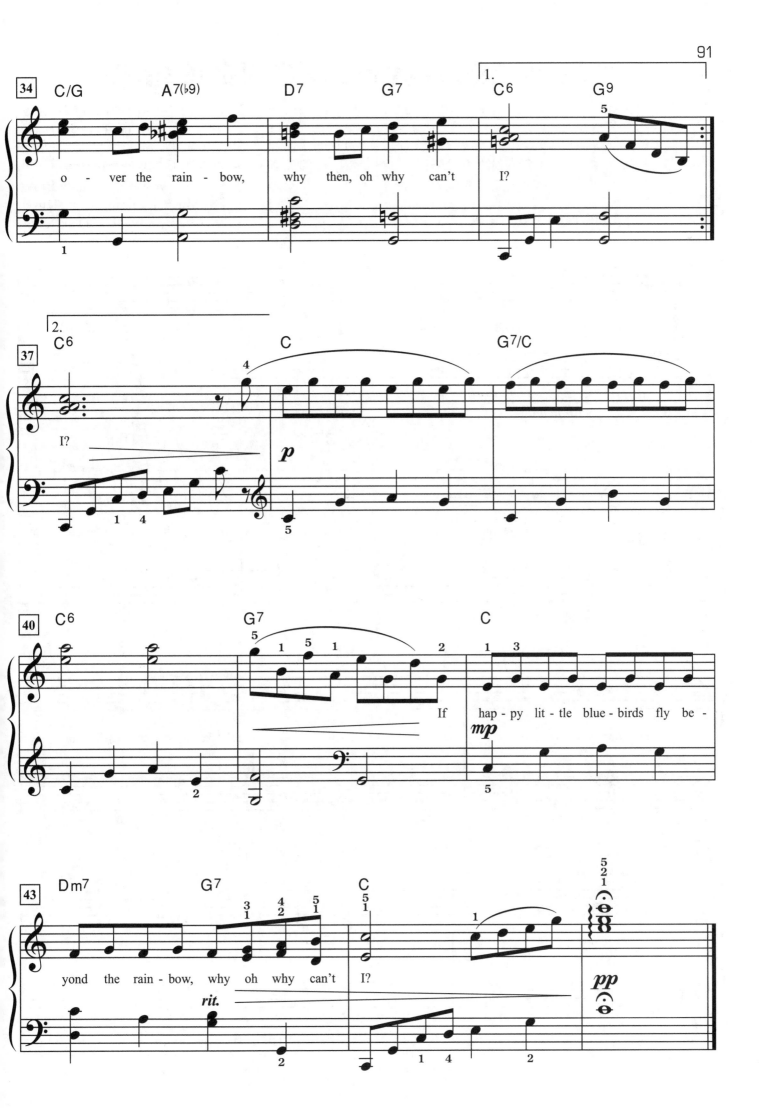

POLKA DOTS AND MOONBEAMS

"Polka Dots and Moonbeams" was written in 1940 by the songwriting team of Johnny Burke and Jimmy Van Heusen, who began their long-lived collaboration in Hollywood in 1939. They wrote some of the greatest hit tunes of the '30s and '40s including the songs for many of legendary actor/singer Bing Crosby's best-known films, highlights of which include "Moonlight Becomes You" (*Road to Morocco*, 1942), "Personality" (*Road to Utopia*, 1945), and "Swinging on a Star" (see p. 115) (*Going My Way*, 1944).

Words by Johnny Burke
Music by Jimmy Van Heusen
Arranged by Dan Coates

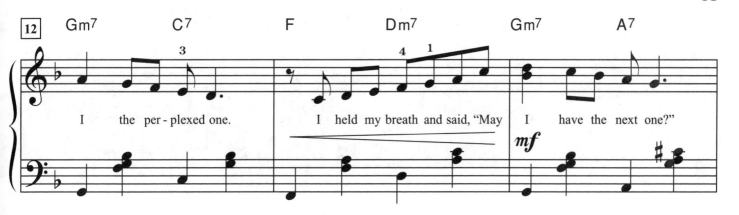

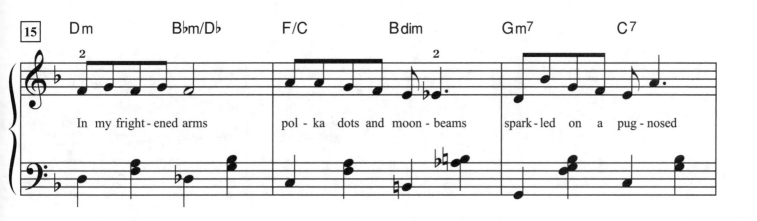

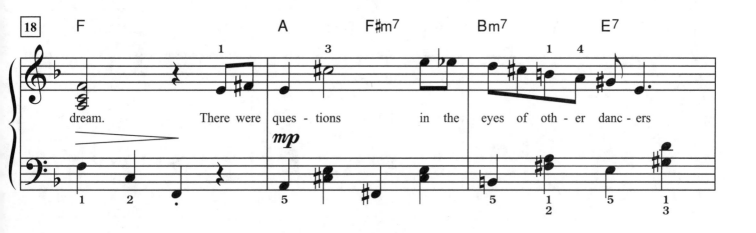

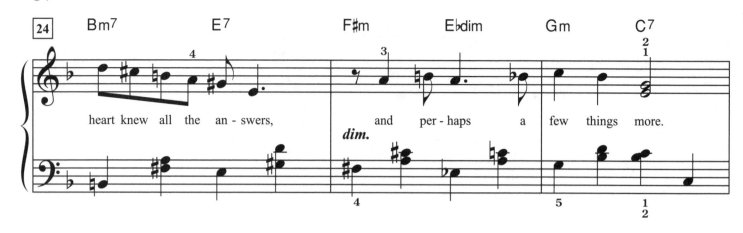

heart knew all the an-swers, and per-haps a few things more.

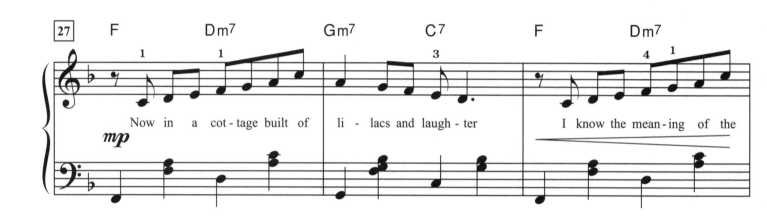

Now in a cot-tage built of li-lacs and laugh-ter I know the mean-ing of the

words "ev-er af-ter." And I'll al-ways see pol-ka dots and moon-beams

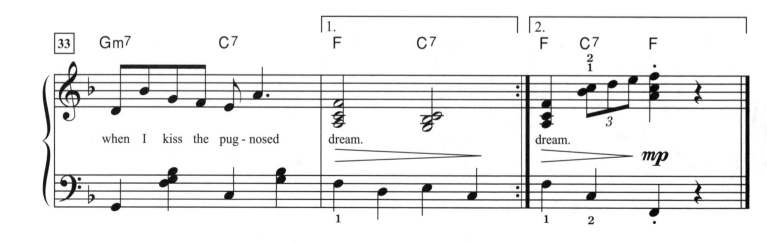

when I kiss the pug-nosed dream. dream.

SHANGRI-LA

Shangri-La is a fictional utopia described in British author James Hilton's novel *Lost Horizon* (1933). In the 1930s and 1940s, the term was used as a slang phrase for heaven or paradise. Carl Sigman, Matt Malneck, and Robert Maxwell wrote a love song based on it in 1946, which became a hit for The Four Coins and also for The Lettermen.

Words and Music by
Carl Sigman, Matt Malneck and Robert Maxwell
Arranged by Dan Coates

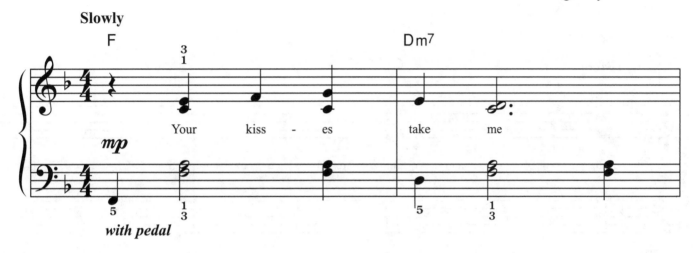

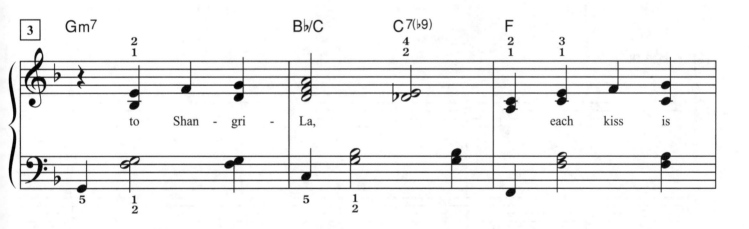

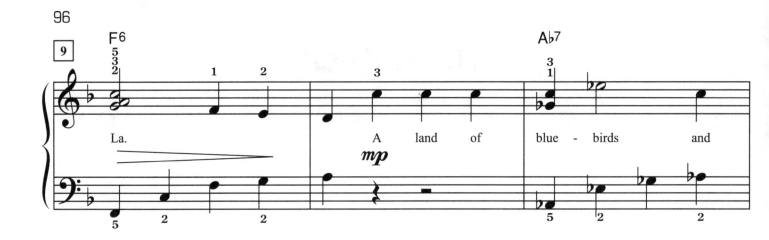

La. A land of blue - birds and

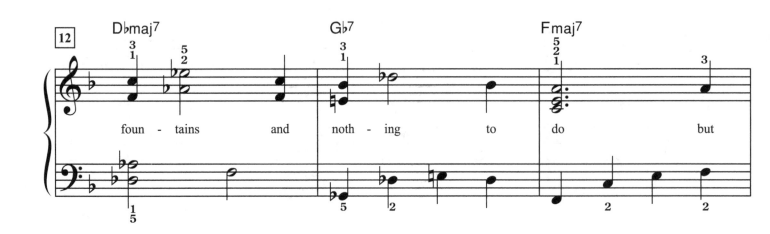

foun - tains and noth - ing to do but

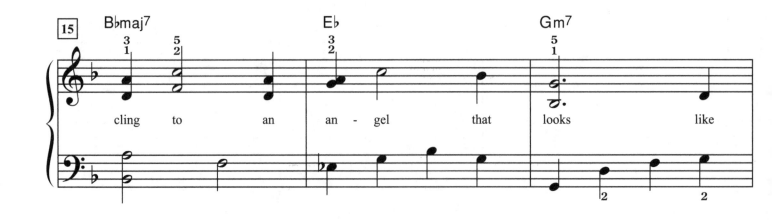

cling to an an - gel that looks like

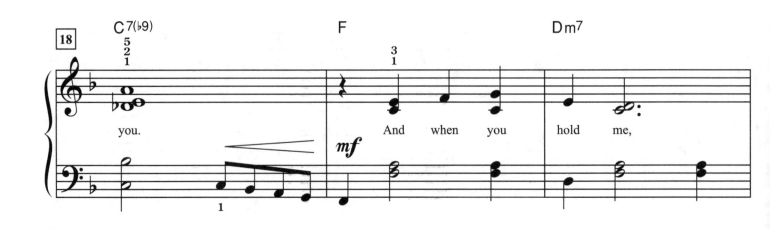

you. And when you hold me,

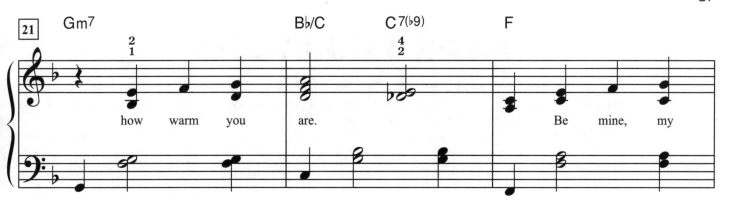

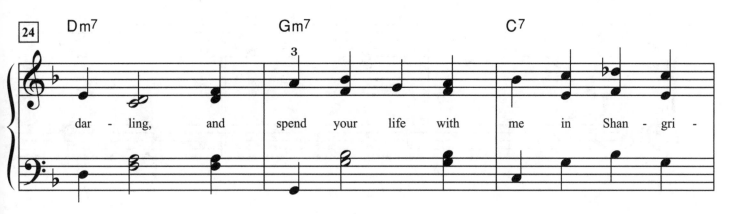

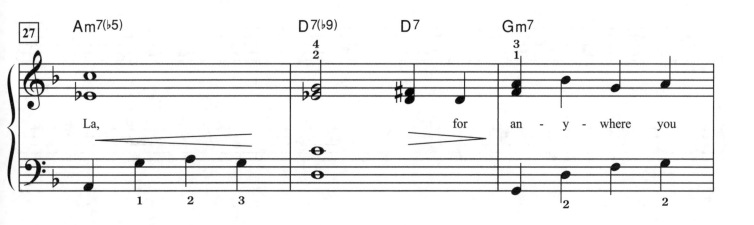

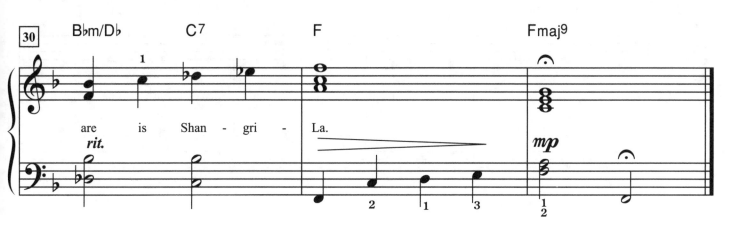

RUM AND COCA-COLA

"Rum and Coca-Cola" (1945) was a popular calypso song which was another big hit for The Andrews Sisters (see page 38). Despite a controversial copyright history and being banned from network radio stations for mentioning alcohol, the song was hugely popular and spent 10 weeks at the top of the Billboard charts.

Music by Jeri Sullavan and Paul Baron
Lyrics by Morey Amsterdam
Additional Lyrics by Al Stillman
Arranged by Dan Coates

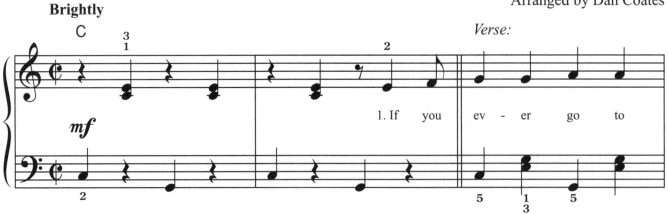

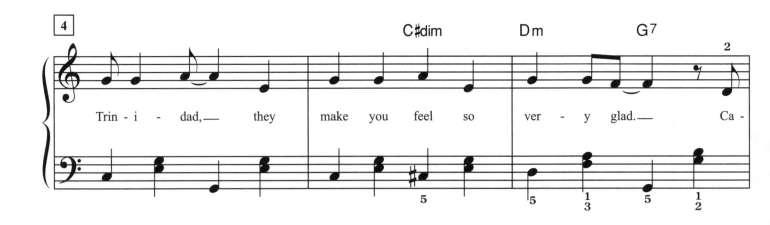

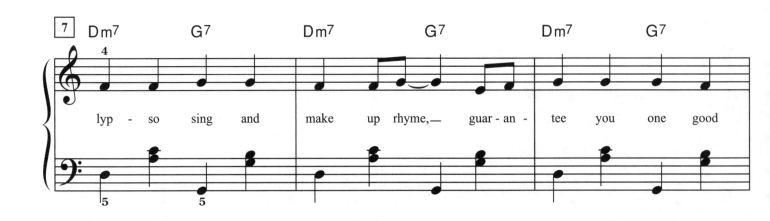

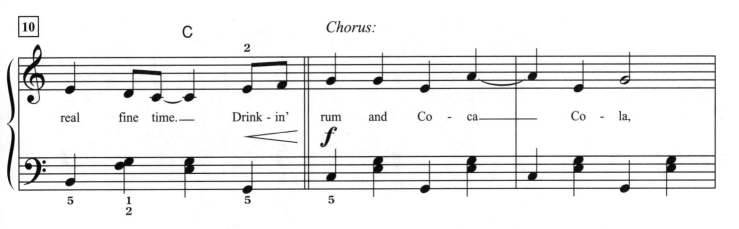

10 **C** *Chorus:*

real fine time.— Drink-in' rum and Co - ca — Co - la,

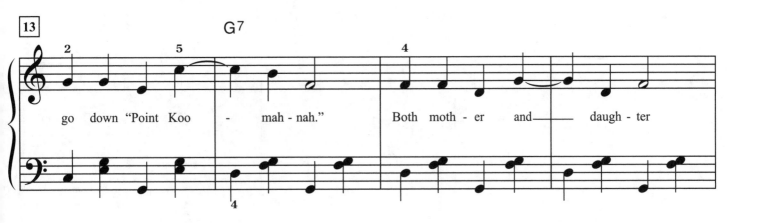

13 **G7**

go down "Point Koo - mah - nah." Both moth - er and— daugh - ter

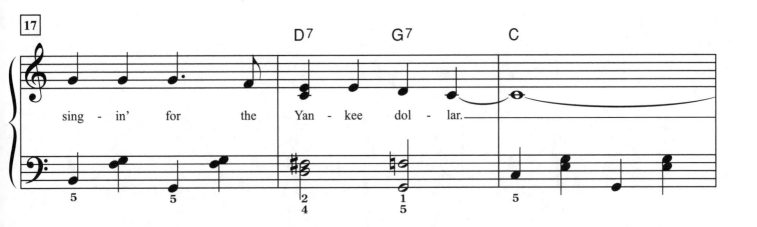

17 **D7** **G7** **C**

sing - in' for the Yan - kee dol - lar.—

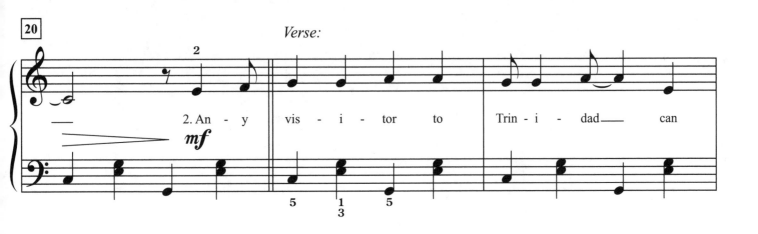

20 *Verse:*

— 2. An - y vis - i - tor to Trin - i - dad— can

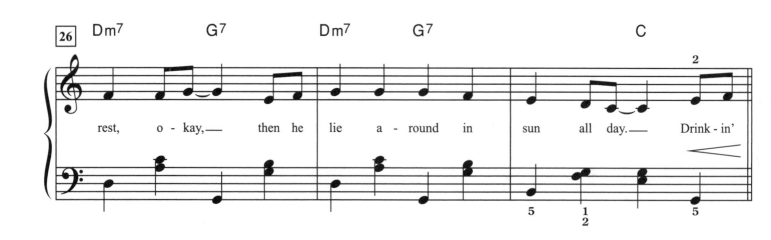

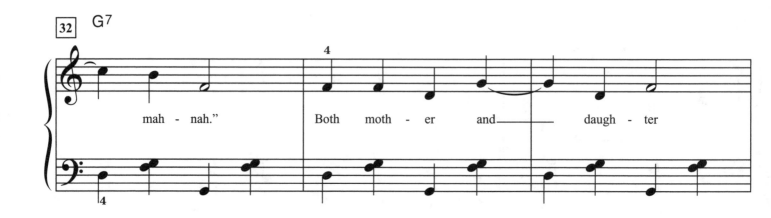

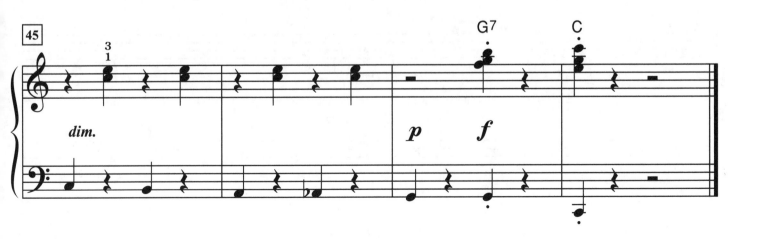

SKYLARK

"Skylark" was written by Johnny Mercer and Hoagy Carmichael in 1942 and was recorded by Glenn Miller, Dinah Shore, and Helen Forrest. It has since become a popular jazz standard. Skylarks have been an inspiration to many composers and writers including Percy Shelley ("To a Skylark"), Ralph Vaughan Williams ("The Lark Ascending"), and others.

Words by Johnny Mercer
Music by Hoagy Carmichael
Arranged by Dan Coates

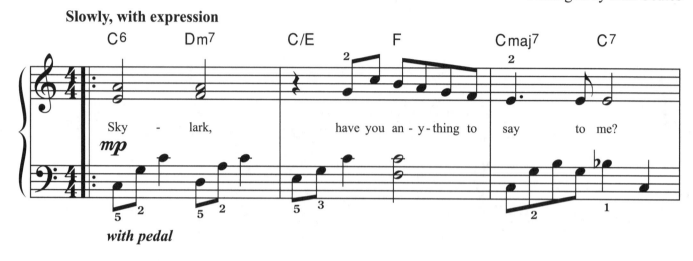

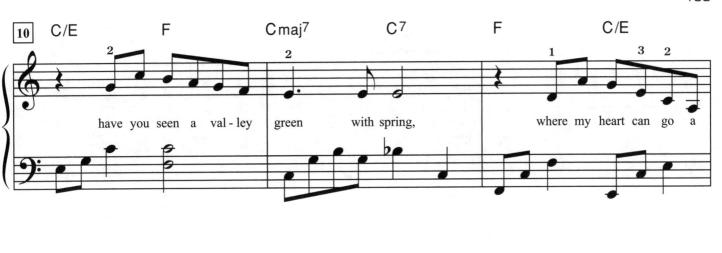

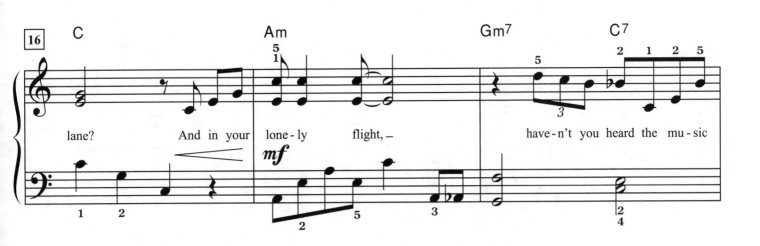

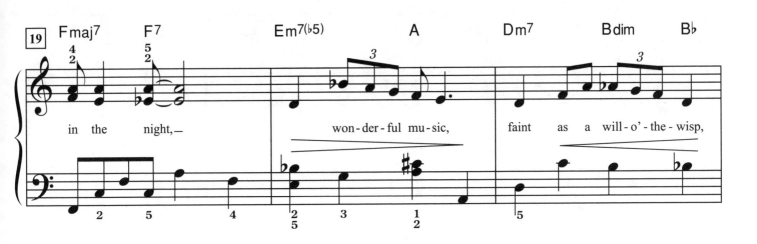

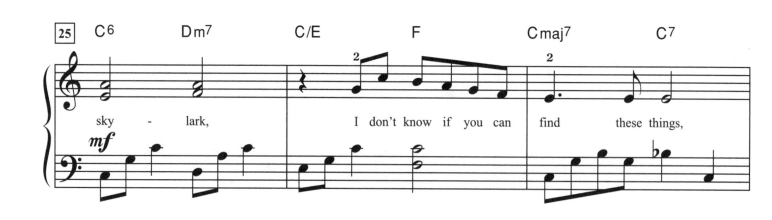

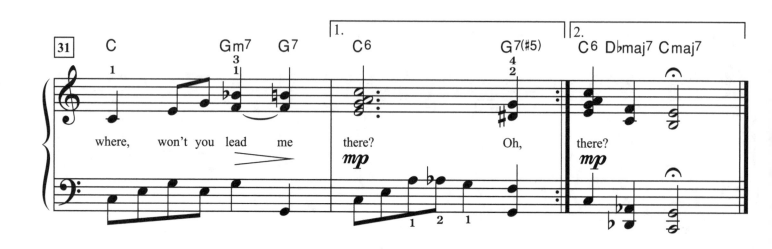

SO IN LOVE

"So In Love" is from Cole Porter's 1948 musical *Kiss Me, Kate*, a comeback for Porter who had experienced a string of unsuccessful songs and musicals following an equestrian accident he had suffered in 1937. The show was based on Shakespeare's *The Taming of the Shrew* and won numerous Tony Awards including the very first Tony Award for Best Musical.

Words and Music by Cole Porter
Arranged by Dan Coates

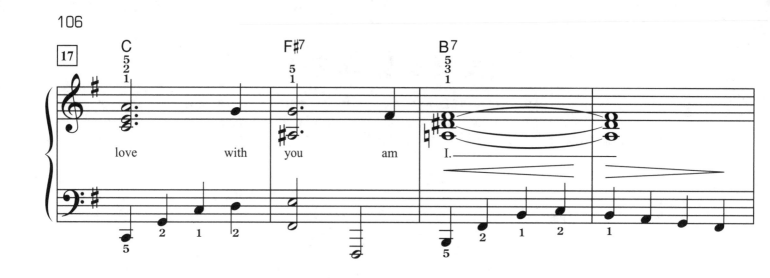

love   with   you   am   I.

Ev - en _____ with - out   you, _____   my

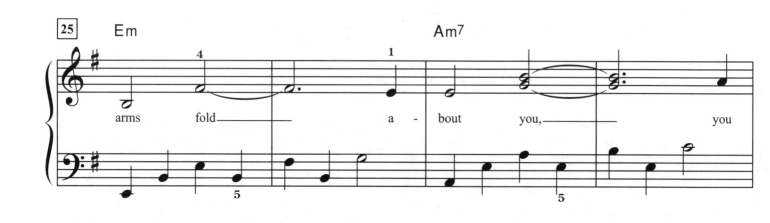

arms   fold _____   a - bout   you, _____   you

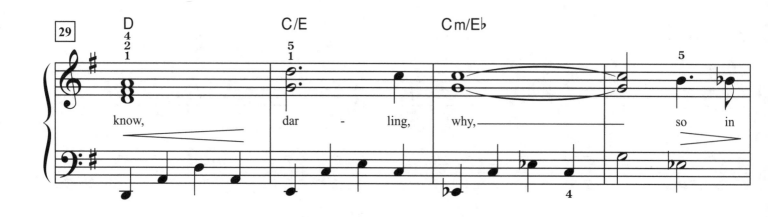

know,   dar - ling,   why, _____   so   in

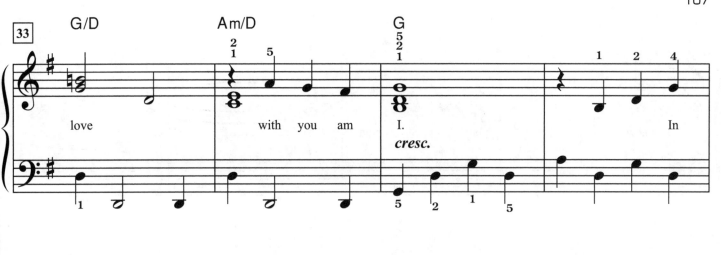

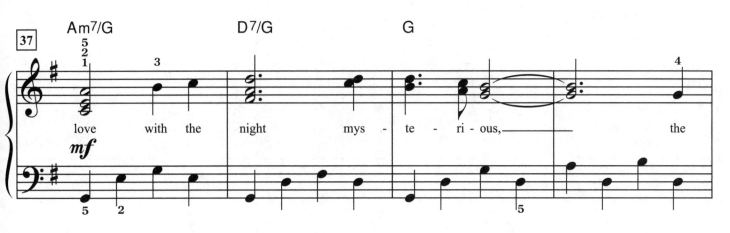

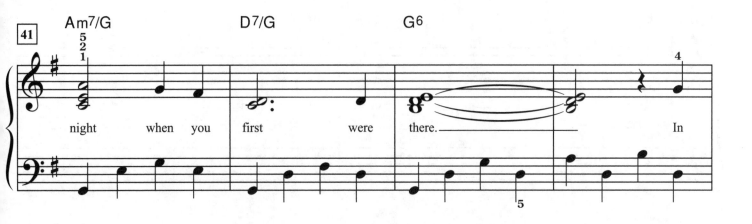

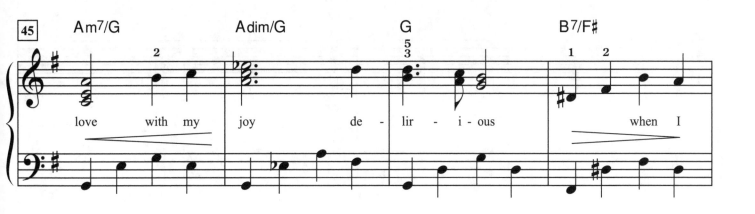

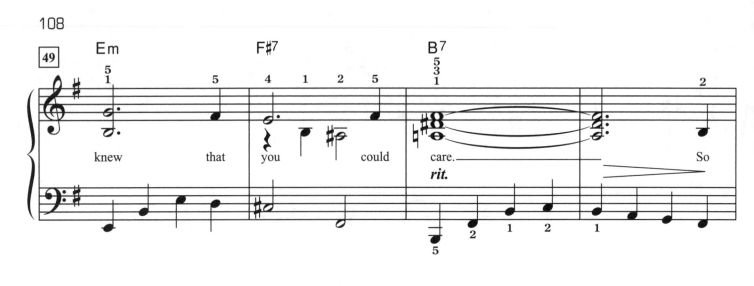

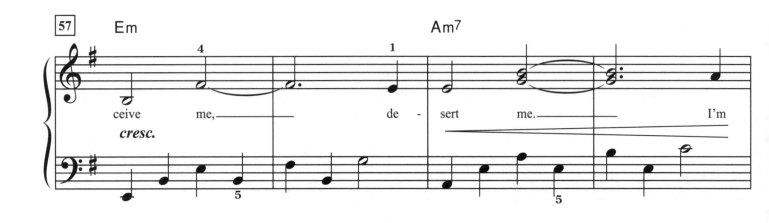

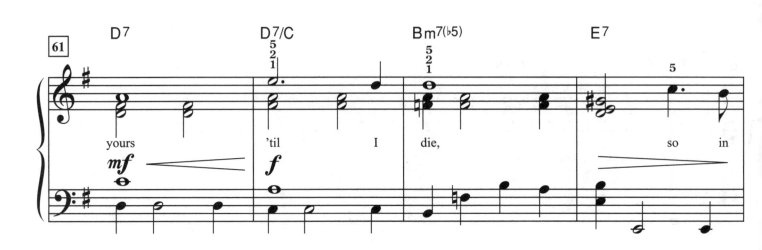

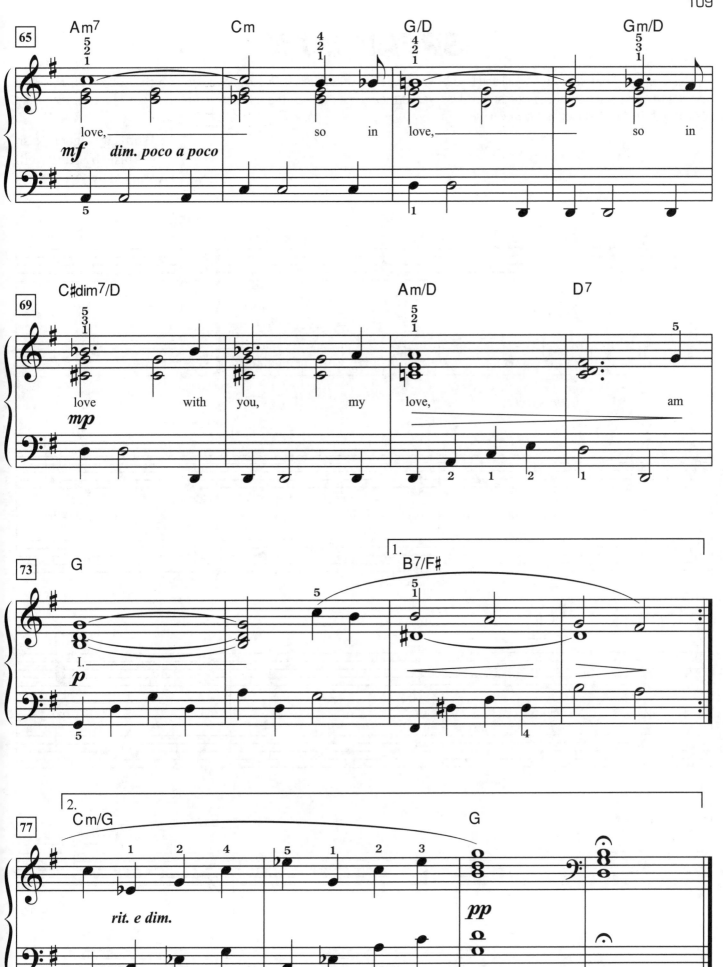

SPEAK LOW

"Speak Low" was written by Kurt Weill and Ogden Nash for the 1943 musical *One Touch of Venus*, a show about a barber who falls in love with a statue of the Roman goddess Venus that comes to life. The opening line of the song is a quotation from Shakespeare's *Much Ado about Nothing*.

Words by Ogden Nash
Music by Kurt Weill
Arranged by Dan Coates

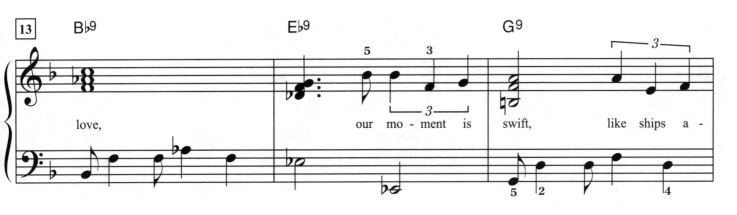

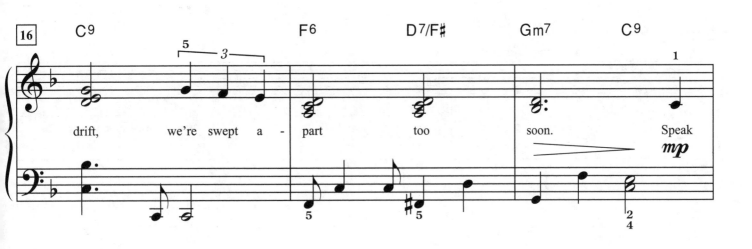

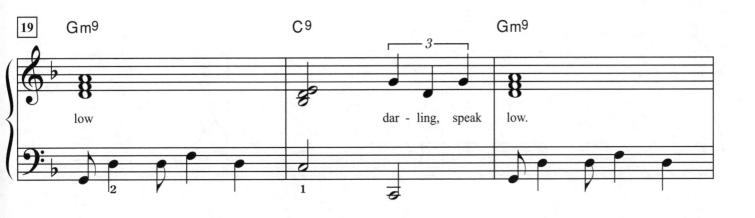

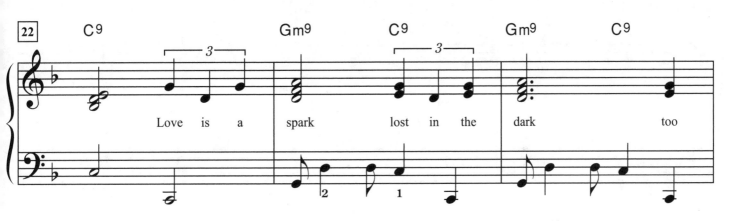

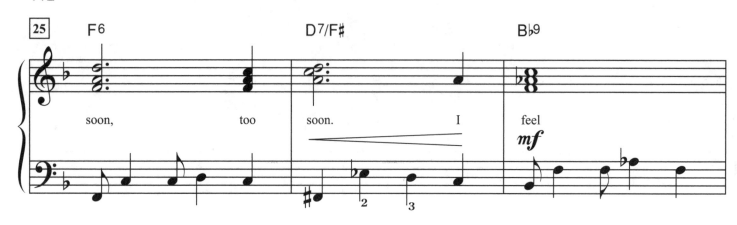

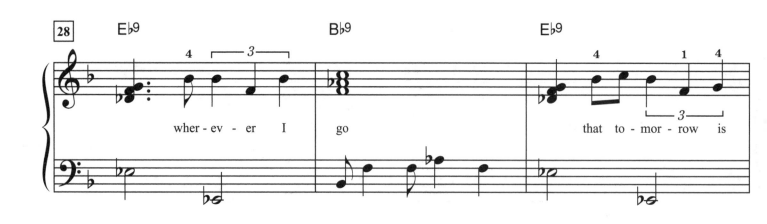

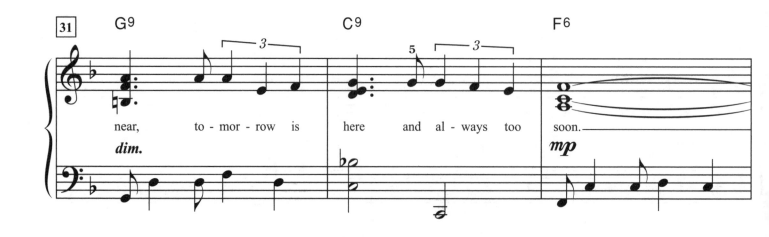

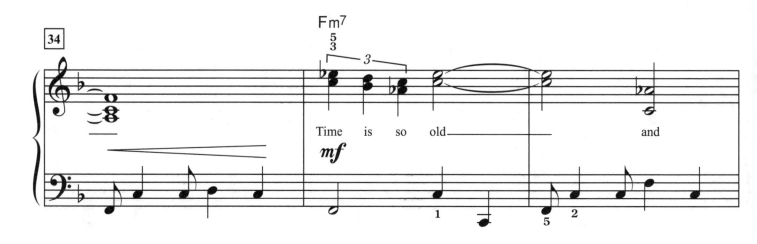

love   so   brief,   love is pure gold_____

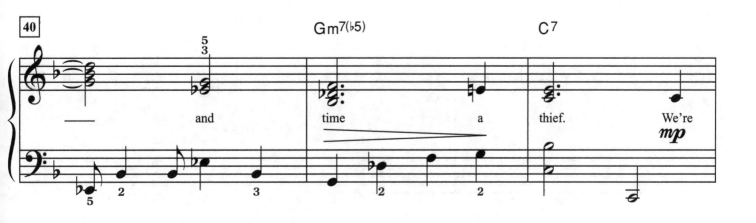

___   and   time   a   thief.   We're

late   dar - ling, we're   late.

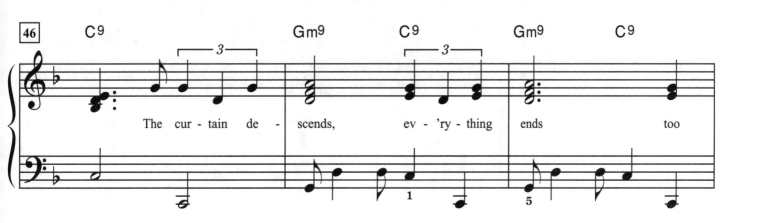

The cur - tain de - scends,   ev - 'ry - thing   ends   too

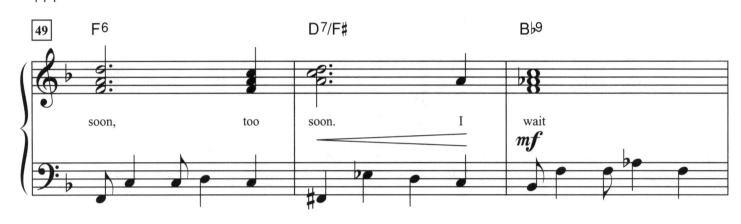

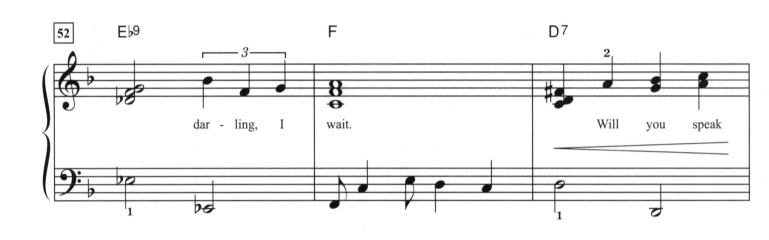

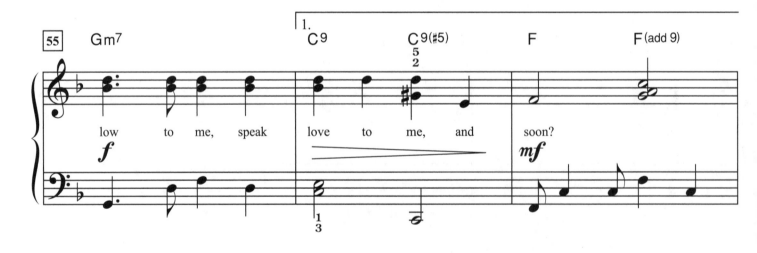

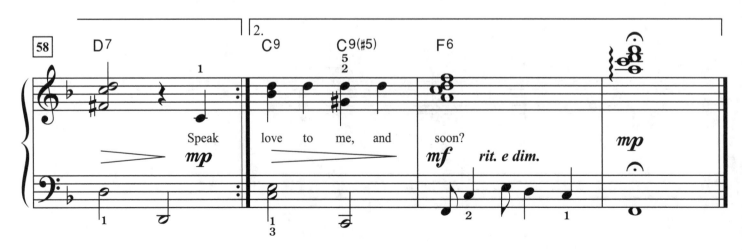

SWINGING ON A STAR

One evening during the filming of Bing Crosby's *Going My Way*, Jimmy Van Heusen was having dinner at Crosby's home. At one point during the night, Crosby reprimanded one of his children for complaining about going to school: "If you don't go to school, you might grow up to be a mule. Do you want that?" Van Heusen loved this line and, with his songwriting partner Johnny Burke, turned it into "Swinging on a Star" for Crosby's film. (Crosby plays a priest who sings the song to a group of troublesome children.) Crosby recorded it in 1944 and since then it has been covered by many great artists including Oscar Peterson, Julie Andrews, and Tony Bennett, to name a few. It won the 1944 Academy Award for Best Original Song, and was inducted into the Grammy Hall of Fame in 2002.

Words by Johnny Burke
Music by Jimmy Van Heusen
Arranged by Dan Coates

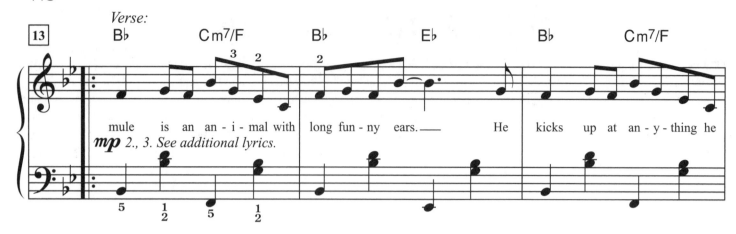

Verse 2:

A pig is an animal with dirt on his face.
His shoes are a terrible disgrace.
He's got no manners when he eats his food.
He's fat and lazy and extremely rude.
But if you don't care a feather or a fig,
you may grow up to be a pig.
Or would you like to swing on a star,
carry moonbeams home in a jar,
and be better off than you are?
Or would you rather be a fish?

Verse 3:

A fish won't do anything but swim in a brook.
He can't write his name or read a book.
To fool the people is his only thought.
Although he's slippery, he still gets caught.
But then if that sort of life is what you wish,
you may grow up to be a fish.
And all the monkeys aren't in the zoo.
Ev'ry day you meet quite a few.
So you see, it's all up to you.
You can be better than you are.

A STRING OF PEARLS

The F. W. Woolworth company was a retail company that was one of the original American five-and-dime stores. Founded in 1878 by Frank Winfield Woolworth, Woolworth's (as it became known) was one of the first stores to display products for customers to handle without the assistance of a sales clerk. In 1941 while working in Glenn Miller's band, Jerry Gray composed "String of Pearls" which became his most successful song. Lyrics were added by Eddie DeLange that describe a love sparked at Woolworth's.

Music by Jerry Gray
Words by Eddie DeLange
Arranged by Dan Coates

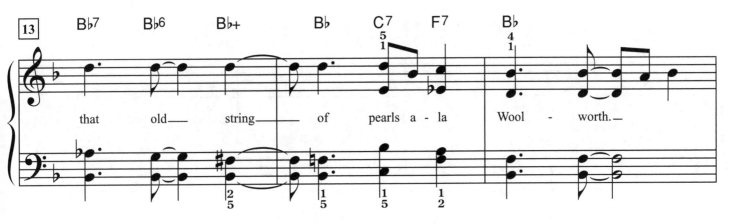

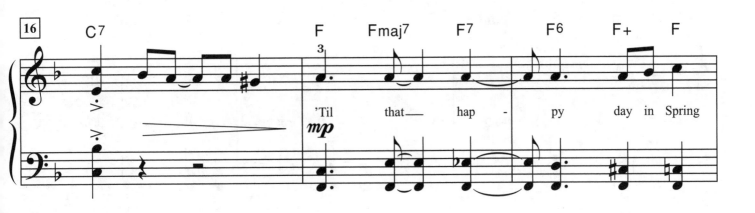

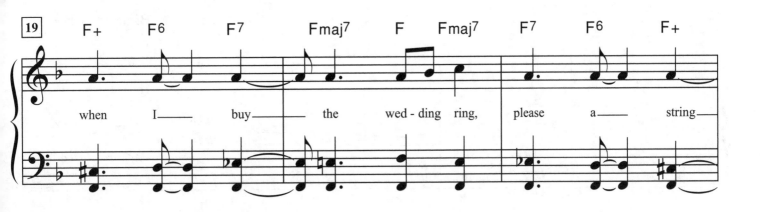

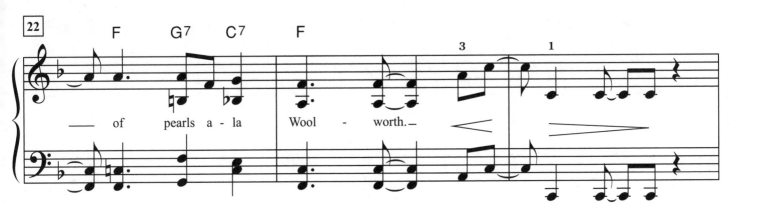

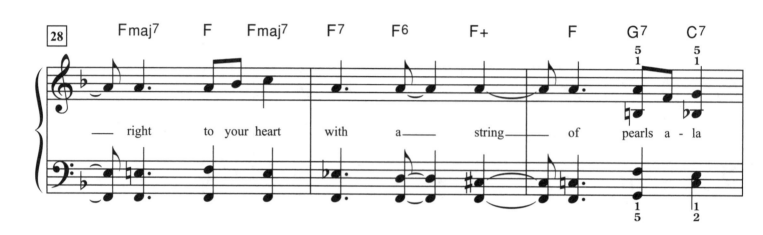

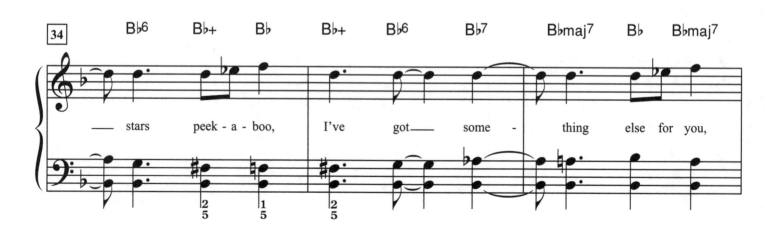

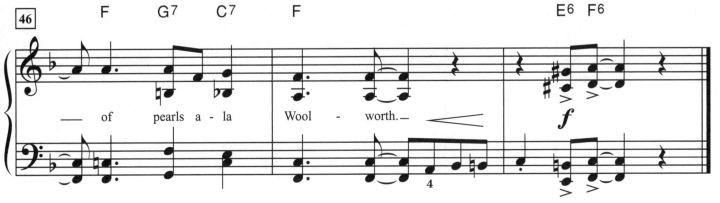

THE SYNCOPATED CLOCK

Leroy Anderson wrote "The Syncopated Clock" for the Boston Pops. He had been invited by Arthur Fiedler, the director of the symphony, to guest conduct for the Pops' annual Harvard night, and he composed the song for the occasion. "The Syncopated Clock" premiered on May 28, 1945, and was recorded for Decca Records in 1950. Additionally, the song was used as the theme music for the WCBS-TV program "The Late Show" for 25 years.

Music by Leroy Anderson
Words by Mitchell Parish
Arranged by Dan Coates

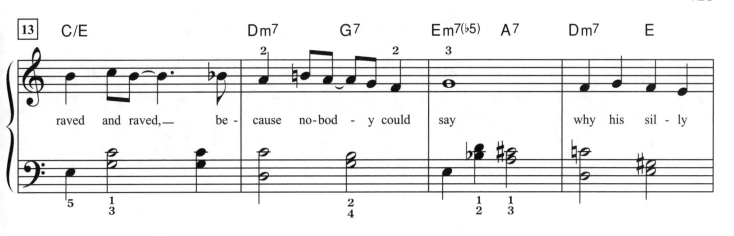

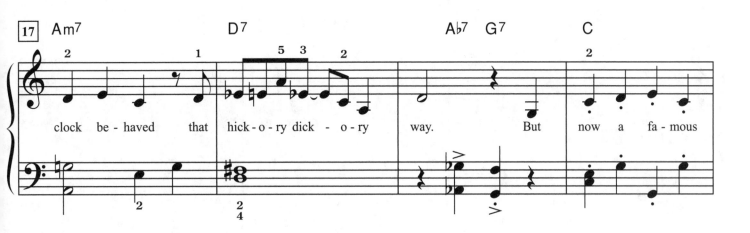

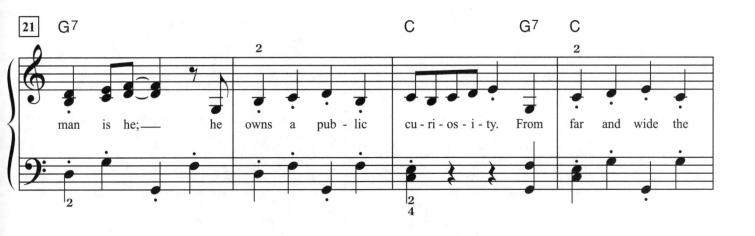

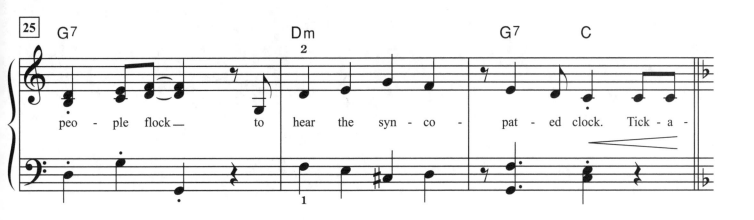

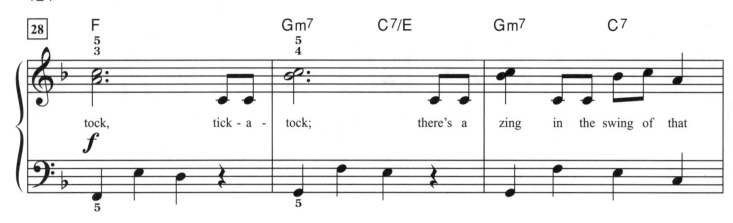

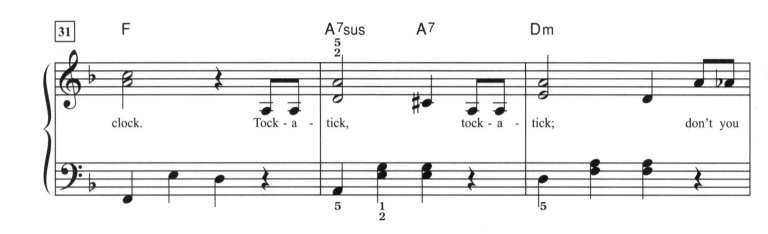

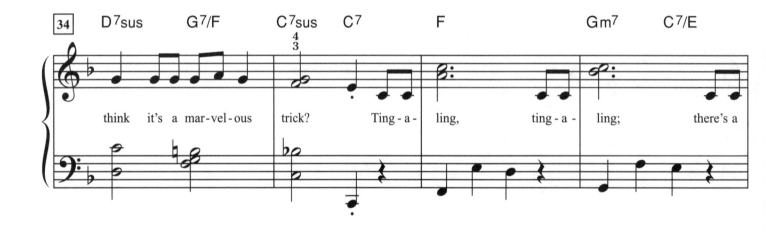

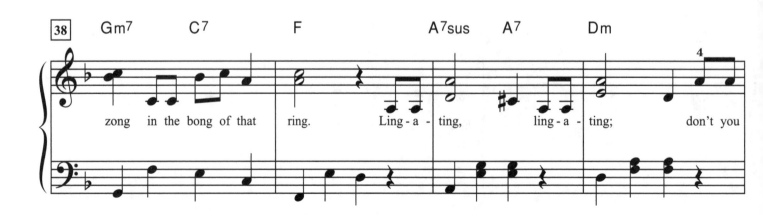

TAKING A CHANCE ON LOVE

"Taking a Chance on Love" is from the 1940 musical *Cabin in the Sky*. The show was based on the Faust legend and was groundbreaking in 1940 for featuring an all African-American cast. MGM adapted it into a film in 1943. The song has become a standard and has been recorded by Dave Brubeck, Rosemary Clooney, Nat King Cole, Ella Fitzgerald, and many others.

Music by Vernon Duke
Words by John Latouche and Ted Fetter
Arranged by Dan Coates

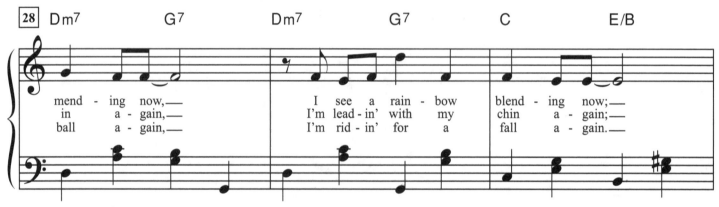

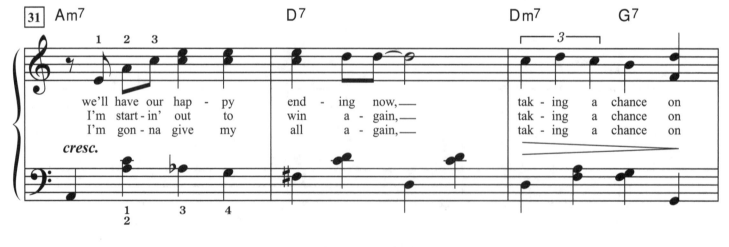

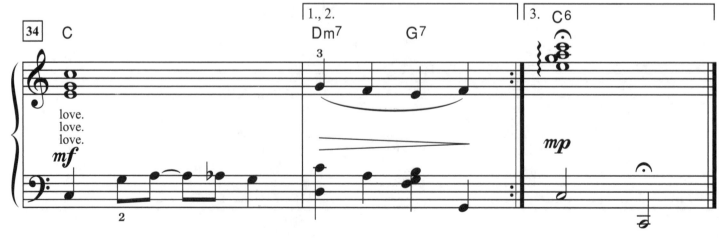

THE TROLLEY SONG

"The Trolley Song" was made famous by Judy Garland in the 1944 film *Meet Me in St. Louis*. The movie was adapted from a series of short stories published in *The New Yorker* magazine by Sally Benson. The plot tells the story of four sisters living in St. Louis around the time of the 1904 World's Fair. Towards the end of the movie, Garland's character sings another famous song to console one of her sisters—"Have Yourself a Merry Little Christmas."

Music by Ralph Blane
Lyrics by Hugh Martin
Arranged by Dan Coates

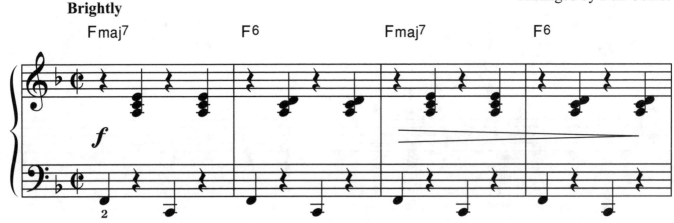

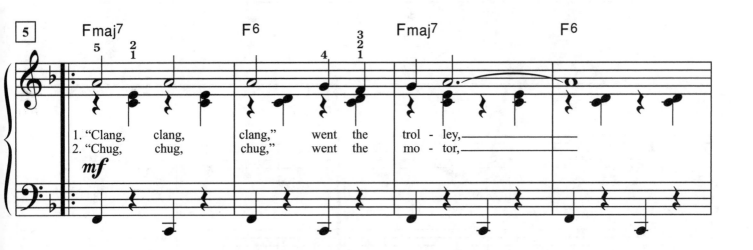

1. "Clang, clang, clang," went the trol - ley,
2. "Chug, chug, chug," went the mo - tor,

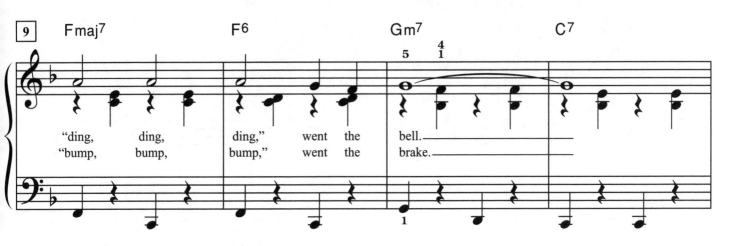

"ding, ding, ding," went the bell.
"bump, bump, bump," went the brake.

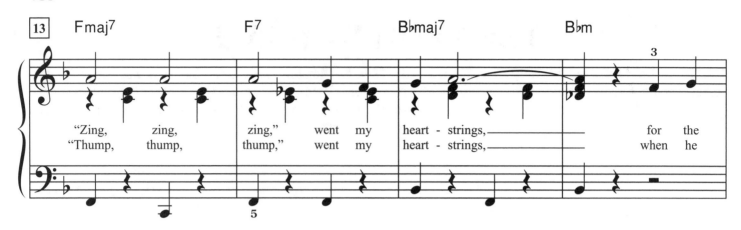

13 Fmaj7   F7   B♭maj7   B♭m

"Zing,   zing,   zing,"   went   my   heart - strings, _____   for   the
"Thump,   thump,   thump,"   went   my   heart - strings, _____   when   he

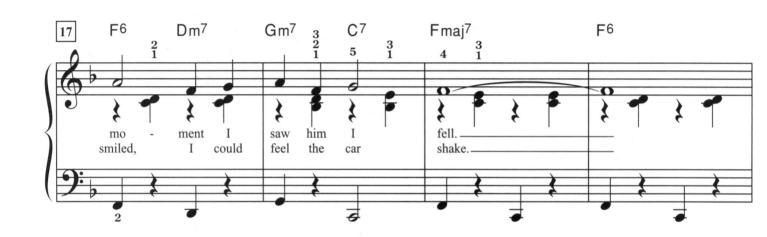

17 F6   Dm7   Gm7   C7   Fmaj7   F6

mo - ment   I   saw   him   I   fell. _____
smiled,   I   could   feel   the   car   shake. _____

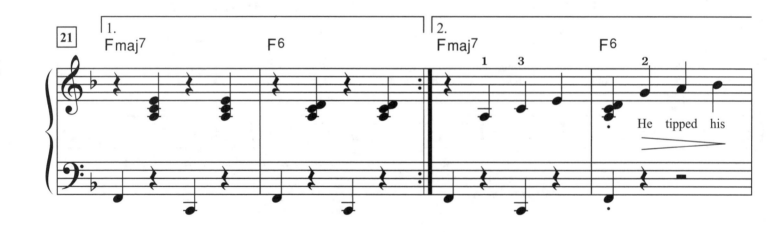

21 1. Fmaj7   F6   2. Fmaj7   F6

He   tipped   his

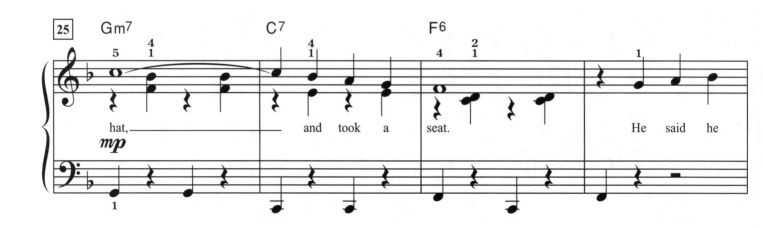

25 Gm7   C7   F6

hat, _____   and   took   a   seat.   He   said   he

mp

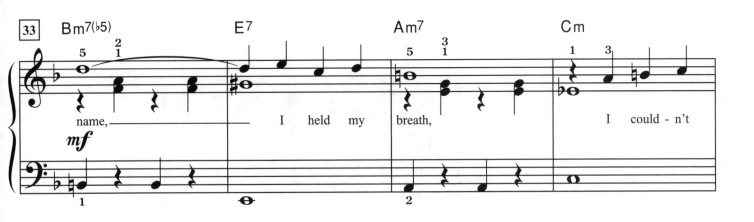

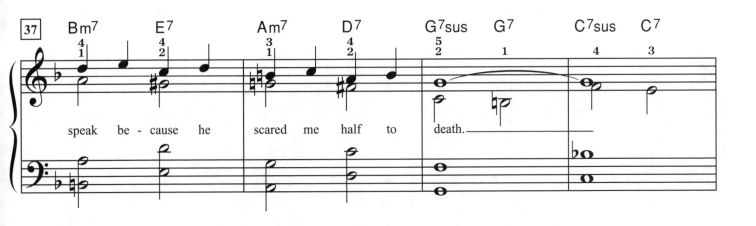

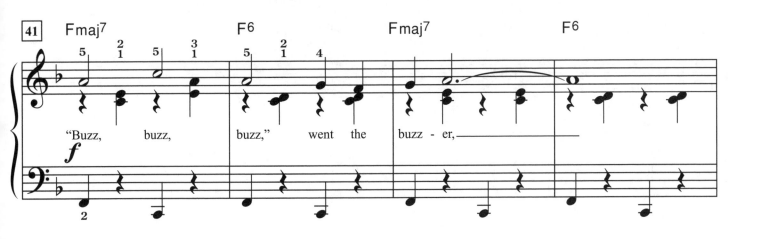

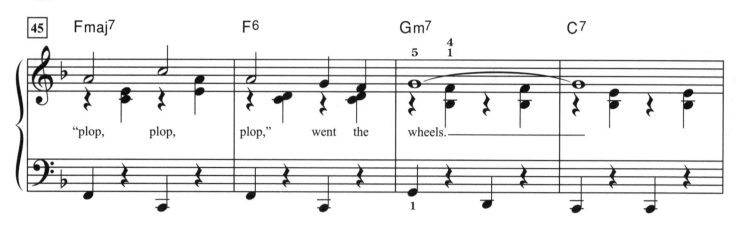

"plop, plop, plop," went the wheels.

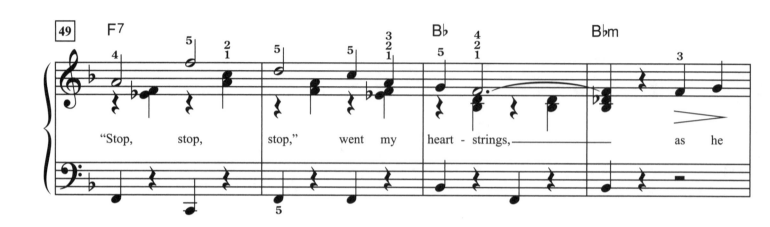

"Stop, stop, stop," went my heart-strings, _____ as he

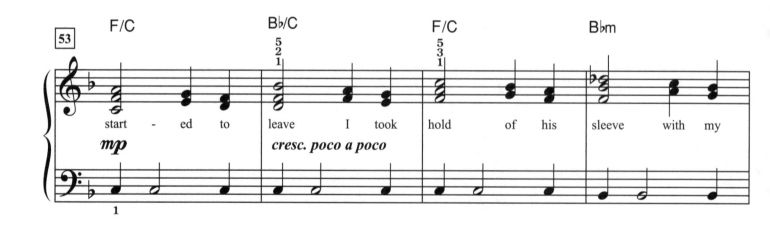

start - ed to leave I took hold of his sleeve with my

mp   *cresc. poco a poco*

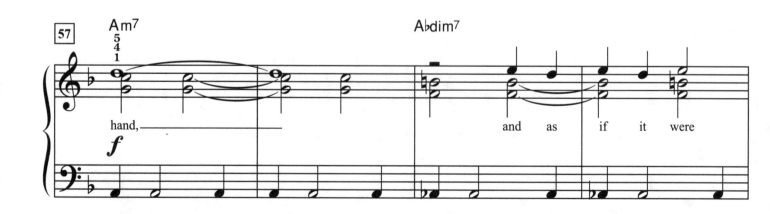

hand, _____ and as if it were

f

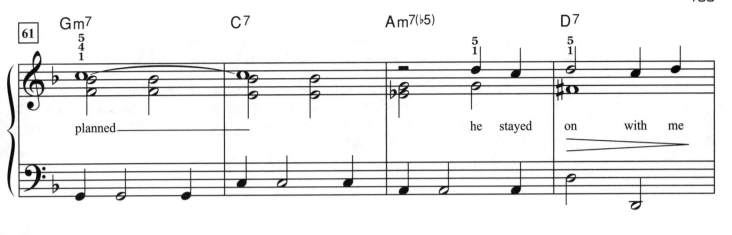

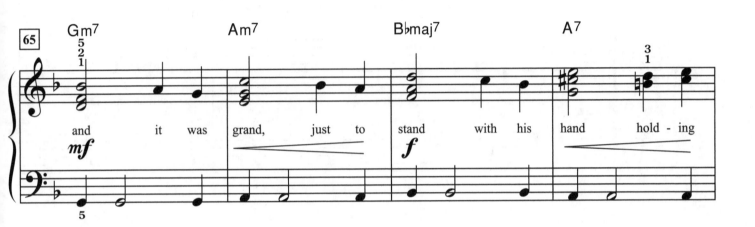

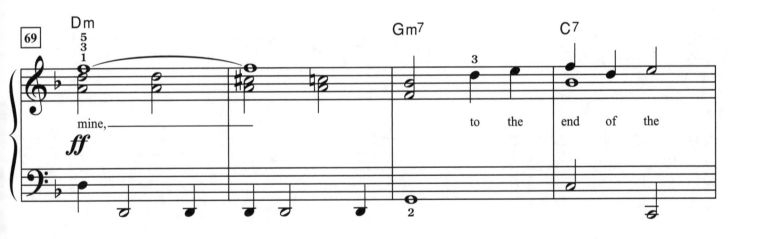

YOU MAKE ME FEEL SO YOUNG

"You Make Me Feel So Young" was composed by Josef Myrow and Mack Gordon in 1946. Myrow was a Russian-born composer who was known in the 1940s and 1950s for his work in film scoring. Gordon was also very successful writing for stage and film, earning nine Oscar nominations for Best Original Song. "You Make Me Feel So Young" has become a standard having been recorded by Rosemary Clooney, Ella Fitzgerald, Frank Sinatra, Mel Tormé, and many others.

Words by Mack Gordon
Music by Josef Myrow
Arranged by Dan Coates

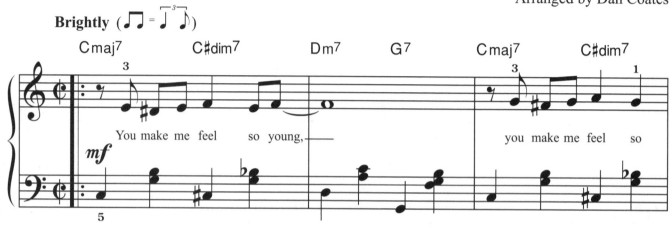

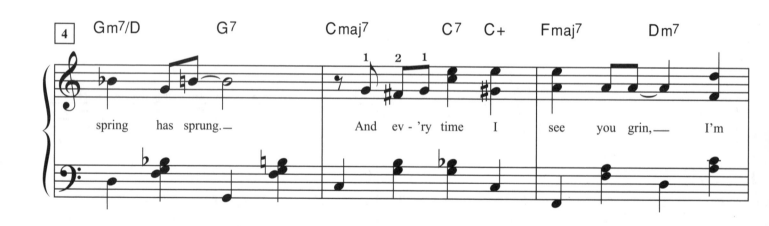

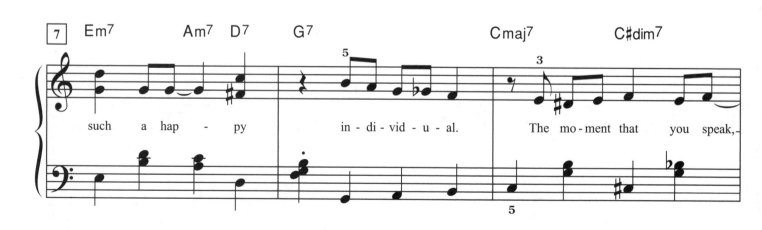

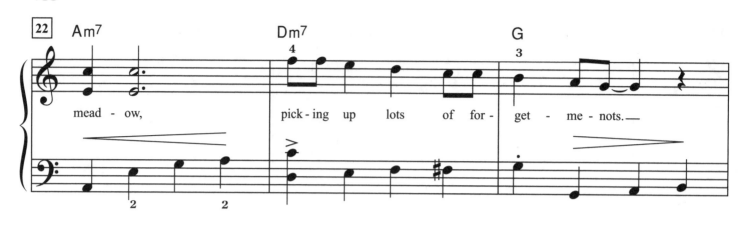

22 Am⁷ — Dm⁷ — G

mead - ow, pick - ing up lots of for - get - me - nots.

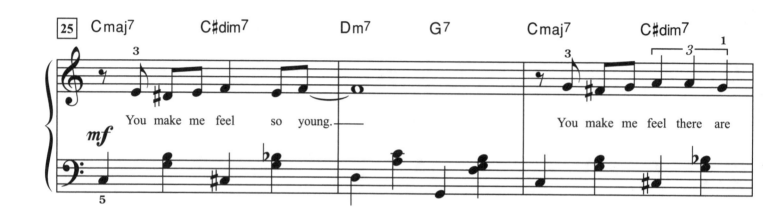

25 Cmaj⁷ — C♯dim⁷ — Dm⁷ — G⁷ — Cmaj⁷ — C♯dim⁷

mf You make me feel so young. You make me feel there are

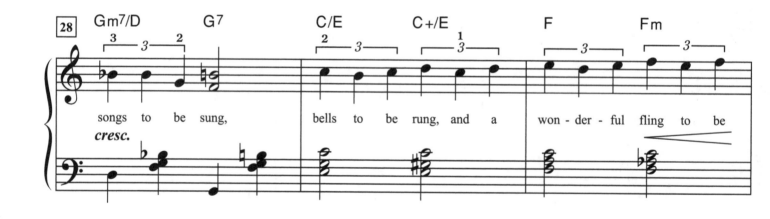

28 Gm⁷/D — G⁷ — C/E — C+/E — F — Fm

cresc. songs to be sung, bells to be rung, and a won - der - ful fling to be

31 C/E — Em⁷ — E♭m⁷ — Dm⁷ — G⁷/F — Em⁷ — Am⁷

flung. And e - ven when I'm old and gray,

YOU'LL NEVER KNOW

"You'll Never Know" was based on a poem written by Dorothy Fern Norris, a young Oklahoma war bride. It was adapted into a song by Harry Warren and Mack Gordon and featured in the film *Hello, Frisco, Hello* (1943). It won the Academy Award that year for Best Original Song.

Lyrics by Mack Gordon
Music by Harry Warren
Arranged by Dan Coates

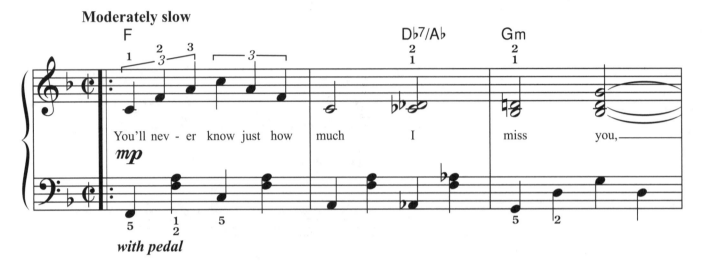

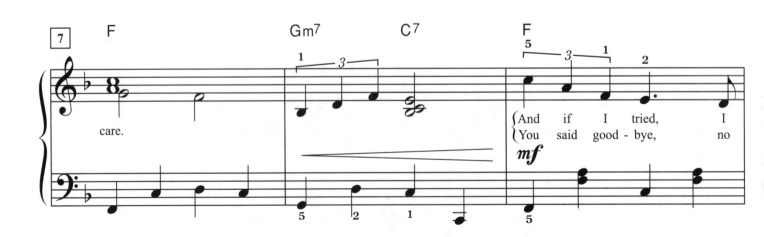

ZIP-A-DEE-DOO-DAH

"Zip-A-Dee-Doo-Dah" is from the Walt Disney film *Song of the South* (1946), which was Disney's first film to feature both live-action and animated scenes. The movie was based on a cycle of stories by Joel Chandler Harris—a Georgia-born journalist of the post-Civil War era—and features Uncle Remus (a kindly, old, story-telling slave) and his fables of Br'er Rabbit (a likable trickster who perpetually finds himself in trouble). "Zip-A-Dee-Doo-Dah" was sung in the film by James Baskett, who played Uncle Remus. It won the 1947 Academy Award for Best Song and has become a Disney classic. Additionally, *Song of the South* is the inspiration for Splash Mountain, the famous water ride at Disney theme parks.

Words by Ray Gilbert
Music by Allie Wrubel
Arranged by Dan Coates

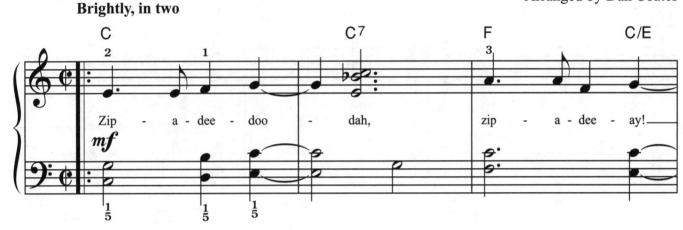

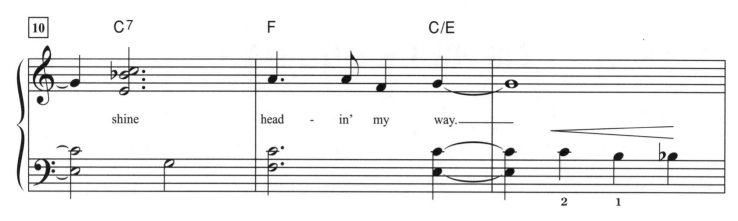

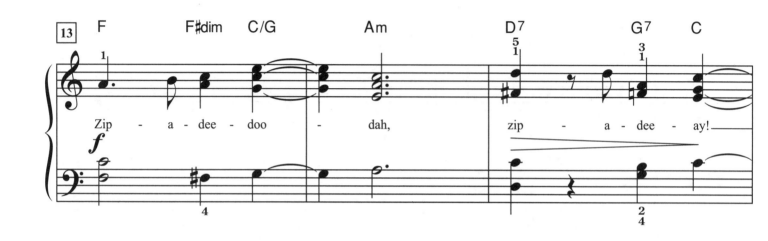

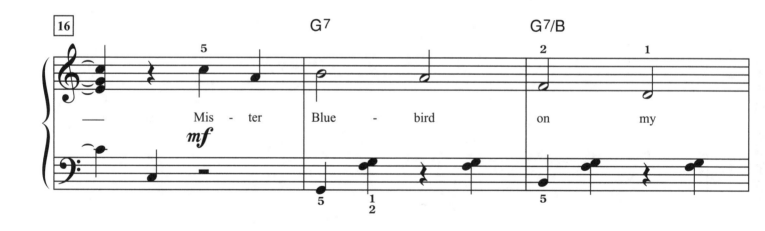